CliffsNotes™

Republic

By Thomas Thornburg, Professor Emeritus, Ball State University

IN THIS BOOK

- Learn about the Life and Background of the Author
- Preview an Introduction to the Work
- Explore concepts and methods of argument in the Critical Commentaries
- Examine in-depth Character Analyses
- Enhance your understanding of the work with Critical Essays
- Reinforce what you learn with CliffsNotes Review
- Find additional information to further your study in CliffsNotes Resource Center and online at www.cliffsnotes.com

D1059720

Wiley Publishing, Inc.

About the Author

Thomas Thornburg is a former Chairman of Humanities and Chairman of University Research at Ball State University.

Publisher's Acknowledgments

Editorial

Project Editor: Tracy Barr

Acquisitions Editor: Greg Tubach

Glossary Editors: The editors and staff at Webster's New World™ Dictionaries

Editorial Administrator: Michelle Hacker

Production

Indexer: York Production Services, Inc.

Proofreader: York Production Services, Inc.

Wiley Indianapolis Composition Services

CliffsNotes™ *Republic*

Published by:

Wiley Publishing, Inc.

909 Third Avenue

New York, NY 10022

www.wiley.com

Table of Contents

How to Use This Book

CliffsNotes *Republic* supplements the original work, giving you background information about the author, an introduction to the work, critical commentaries, expanded glossaries, and a comprehensive index. CliffsNotes Review tests your comprehension of the original text and reinforces learning with questions and answers, practice projects, and more. For further information on Plato and the *Republic*, check out the CliffsNotes Resource Center.

CliffsNotes provides the following icons to highlight essential elements of particular interest:

Reveals the underlying themes in the work.

Helps you to more easily relate to or discover the depth of a character.

Uncovers elements such as setting, atmosphere, mystery, passion, violence, irony, symbolism, tragedy, foreshadowing, and satire.

Enables you to appreciate the nuances of words and phrases.

Don't Miss Our Web Site

Discover classic literature as well as modern-day treasures by visiting the CliffsNotes Web site at www.cliffsnotes.com. You can obtain a quick download of a CliffsNotes title, purchase a title in print form, browse our catalog, or view online samples.

You'll also find interactive tools that are fun and informative, links to interesting Web sites, tips, articles, and additional resources to help you, not only for literature, but for test prep, finance, careers, computers, and the Internet too. See you at www.cliffsnotes.com!

LIFE AND BACKGROUND OF THE AUTHOR

Plato's World

Plato is often referred to as a Greek, and indeed his native language was Greek, and he was born in the part of Europe that is today the country of Greece. In Plato's time, however, there was no such country. Instead, on the peninsula and islands of today's Greece, there were a number of *city-states* (walled cities and the outlying rural areas and villages that each could defend) that were governed independently of each other, although groups of them were formed into alliances, variously strong or weak, and were governed in vastly different ways, according to the history of each. In Plato's day, the greatest of the city-states (if greatness may be defined by level of learning, art and architecture, music, and general quality of life) was Athens. Plato was an Athenian.

If Athens represented a degree of humanistic civilization that had not been seen before in European and Mediterranean culture—and strong arguments can be made that it did—still it was in many ways different from what we today are likely to think of as an enlightened culture. During its relatively brief period of democracy, Athens was governed by its citizens. However, women were not citizens of Athens, nor were slaves. Boys were educated (even some slaves were educated); girls, of course, were not. Most Athenian citizens were literate, but books (handwritten scrolls) were few. Medical knowledge and sanitation were advanced—compared to conditions, for example, in the Europe of the middle ages—but the life span of most people was relatively short. Travel was possible, but was very slow; navigational instruments were relatively primitive, so that ships were forced to sail close to islands and coastlines, and travelers on land (most of whom went by foot) were in constant danger of attack by robbers, for the mountainous country between walled cities was wild and lawless.

Plato's Early Life

Plato was born in 428 or 427 B.C. Both his mother and father were members of wealthy and politically powerful families in Athens, which was at the time of Plato's birth embroiled in a political upheaval involving the city-states of Athens and Sparta and their allies. This political unrest had recently manifested itself (431 B.C.) in the outbreak of armed hostilities and the commencement of a disastrous civil war, the Peloponnesian War (431–404 B.C.). This war shattered the Athenian Empire, practically destroyed the governments of all the Greek city-states, and resulted in anarchy (a kind of mob-rule) in 404–403 B.C.

Thus Plato grew to young adulthood surrounded by the strife of civil war, and he witnessed several revolutions in Athens: He saw a government of democrats (the rule of the many) replaced by an oligarchy (the rule of the chosen few), which was then again replaced by the democrats. Plato tells us in a letter he wrote when he was 60 that, in his youth, he had hoped to become actively involved in politics, chiefly because he thought it was his social responsibility, but also because many of Plato's friends and relatives had invited him to help them to govern the Athenians and to share in the exercise of political power. But the young Plato decided to defer his political allegiance until he could observe his friends and relatives in action. Once the young Plato had seen the various political factions conducting what seemed to him nothing more than self-serving policies, motivated by simple greed and an appetite for absolute power over the people—rather than exercising government *for* the people and their welfare—Plato was disappointed, shocked by the violence he saw done to the people, and finally disgusted with all the parties involved.

Plato's Growth as a Philosopher

It was after his introduction to the common corruption of the Athenian political world that Plato began to have second thoughts about his place in such a world; it was during this time that Plato began seriously to consider how the interests and well-being of a people could best be served by the citizens who govern them. And it was at this time in his growth as a thinker that a singular event occurred: Plato witnessed a series of politically motivated maneuvers and fabrications brought against his old friend and teacher, Socrates. Plato saw very clearly that the charges brought against Socrates were unjust; it is plain that Plato feared for the outcome of those charges. How, Plato wondered, could justice be achieved for Socrates; indeed, how might justice be achieved for every citizen of the state? It is this interest in the possibility of achieving justice for every citizen that serves as the major argument in the *Republic*, an interest which threads through every political dialogue that Plato wrote.

It is plain that Plato must have known and listened to Socrates during Plato's childhood and young adulthood (Plato's relatives, Critias and Charmides, were friends of Socrates). When Plato was 27 or 28, his friends and relatives who had invited him to join them in governing the Athenians tried to get even with some of their political enemies whom they had overthrown in their latest revolution. They tried, Plato tells us, to enlist the aid of old Socrates in helping them to arrest one of their political adversaries and to carry him off and execute him. Apparently the attempt to involve Socrates in this travesty of justice and subsequent murder in the name of the state was in order to lend the name of the great philosopher as a party to their illegal activity and to force him to share in their guilt. Socrates refused, and his refusal to ally himself with corrupt politicians was remarked and noted. But even when the political power bases shifted and a new revolution ensued, Plato was tempted to involve himself in politics, whereupon he saw the same system of political pay-backs and corruptions practiced by the "new" leaders of the state. And Socrates' steadfast refusal to deal with corrupt politicians, no matter their party affiliation, had not gone unnoticed.

Socrates is one of the most singular men in history: He was a great teacher, but he never was employed as a teacher, never took money for the things he taught. He never wrote anything so far as we know; all we know of what he taught was recorded by his "students," the young men of Athens whom he met on various street corners in Athens, youngsters (like Plato) whom he engaged in conversations. For Socrates was a true philosopher, a lover of learning and of truth.

As we have seen, Socrates refused to ally himself for any reason with people whom he felt clearly to be culpable of unjust acts. And Socrates would not cease asking questions of those same people: What is your understanding of justice? If you are wise, how do you know you are wise? If you are a leader of the state, where precisely are you leading the state? If you are in a position of authority, what are your credentials for that authority? In short, Socrates by his own precepts and example must have encouraged the youth of Athens, including Plato, to question authority wherever that authority might reside. In the turbulent Athens of his day, this led to Socrates' downfall.

Socrates, known as the gadfly of Athens because of his persistent questions about the authenticity of many "truths," was in 399 B.C. brought to trial and charged with not believing in the gods and with corrupting the youth of Athens. Socrates had made too many enemies in high places. At a time when the young Plato was still considering becoming a politician, his dear friend and dearest teacher was put to death by politicians. The story of Socrates' trial and death is told in Plato's dialogues, the *Apology* and the *Phaedo*.

Thus it is that Plato apparently decided that he had had enough of politics. He resolved to spend his time in the study of philosophy, like his teacher, Socrates, because Plato believed that a just and uncorrupted state (as a political reality) could not be formed until citizens arrived at an understanding of what constitutes *justice* and the *good life* as concepts. Plato resolved to dedicate his life to the study of philosophy.

After the death of Socrates, Plato left Athens and, according to Hermodorus, one of Plato's students, he spent the next few years traveling in Greece, Egypt, and Italy. Again, the letter that Plato wrote when he was 60 (*The Seventh Letter*) tells us that he went to Italy and Sicily when he was 40, but the gluttony and sexual debauchery he found there disgusted him. He did make a new friend there, Dion, the brother-in-law of Dionysius I of Syracuse (in Sicily).

Plato's Academy

In 387 or 386 B.C., Plato returned to Athens and founded the Academy, which was intended to serve as a school for future leaders of state. Plato apparently planned the curriculum of the Academy (primarily courses in philosophy, science, and law) to provide for the training of the ideal philosopher-rulers he had described in the *Republic*; we may see the Academy as being the first university. The Academy rapidly became the intellectual center of Greek life. According to Aristotle, who studied with Plato for almost 20 years, Plato lectured without notes, probably engaging his students in conversations after the fashion of his own mentor, Socrates. As the fame of the Academy grew, it attracted many brilliant thinkers to join its faculty, and we are told that Plato sent many of those faculty to help various city-states and colonies to form legislative bodies.

Plato's Later Years

In 367 B.C., when he was 60 years old and at the height of his fame as head of the Academy, Plato heard from his friend Dion of Syracuse, who invited Plato to come and teach the young Dionysius II, who had recently become King of Syracuse. Plato accepted the invitation because he still retained his old wish to become actively involved in politics, to be a man of action as well as a "mere man of words." But Dion soon got into trouble because of political intrigues in Syracuse, and he was banished from the country. Plato again returned to Athens, only to return to Syracuse again in 361 B.C. to help Dionysius II rule fairly and equitably, put the kingdom under a rule of law, and eschew the temptations of tyranny. Plato failed in this endeavor, and he soon found himself in personal danger. After escaping Syracuse, Plato returned home to Athens; he never again meddled directly in political affairs, although several members of his faculty did actively aid Dion's military expedition against Syracuse (Sicily) in 357 B.C., an expedition that overthrew the tyranny there.

By this time, Plato had completed most of the writings for which we remember him, but late in his life, he was still intrigued by the problem of how to accomplish a legislative body that might serve to put into action the ideas and the ideals he had conversed about in such works as the *Republic*. Aristotle, who became a student at the Academy in 367 B.C., tells us that Plato and his students were conversing about the problem of "laws," a recorded system for governing a given state, when Plato died in 348 or 347 B.C.

INTRODUCTION TO THE WORK

Introduction

The *Republic* is arguably the most popular and most widely taught of Plato's writings. Although it contains its dramatic moments and it employs certain literary devices, it is not a play, a novel, a story; it is not, in a strict sense, an essay. It is a kind of extended conversation that embraces a central argument, an argument that is advanced by the proponent of the argument, Socrates. The *Republic* may be seen as a kind of debate, a fitting description for most of the *Dialogues*.

It is Plato's intent in this dialogue to establish, philosophically, the ideal state, a state that would stand as a model for all emerging or existing societies currently functioning during Plato's time and extending into our own times. And we are to infer that any proposed *changes* in the policy of effecting justice in any state would have to meet the criteria of the ideal state: the *Republic*.

Since its first appearance, the *Republic* has traditionally been published in ten books, probably from its having been so divided into ten "books" in its manuscript form. In order to clarify its argument, this Note further subdivides those ten books in its discussion.

The Socratic Method

Socrates' method of engaging conversations with his fellow citizens has come to be known in history as the *Socratic Dialectic* or the *Socratic Method*, and its method of pursuing a given truth is still adopted by many university and public school teachers to the present day. It is the method that Plato adopted for the *Republic* and for all of his *Dialogues* (conversations).

Socrates' (and Plato's) method of opening a dialogue is in almost every instance to pose a question of meaning (to ask for a definition of a term or terms for the sake of forming up a logical argument). For example, Socrates might ask at the outset of a dialogue: "If you claim to be an honest man, how would you define *honesty*?" Or he might ask a person who claimed to be virtuous for a definition of virtue, or a person who claimed to be courageous for a definition of courage. And then Socrates might ask for examples of courageous, or virtuous, or honest behavior; or he might ask for analogues (things similar) to those things. Thus Socrates conversed with the young men of Athens, young men who were apparently disenchanted with their teachers whom their parents had hired and who apparently did not know as much as Socrates knew.

But Socrates, who some claimed to be the wisest man, claimed to know nothing except that every person should carefully determine what he thinks he knows. He said that the unexamined life is not worth living. He taught that men claimed to come to wisdom through poetry and argument and music, when it was plain that they did not even know what they were doing. And he also taught that politicians claimed to serve justice and to sit in judgment on their fellow citizens when at the same time those same politicians and "leaders" of the state could not even define justice and might, in fact, be said to be culpable (guilty) of certain injustices perpetrated against their fellow citizens. How, Socrates asked, can any man claim to serve justice when that same man cannot even *define* justice? The question is still relevant in the twenty-first century.

The Setting for and the Speakers in the Dialogue

As in all of the Platonic dialogues, the participants in the debate are friends or acquaintances of the central speaker, Socrates, and they conduct their conversations in the house of one of the participants. The dialogue in the *Republic* takes place in Cephalus' house; Cephalus is an older man, a wealthy and retired merchant. He has assembled several friends and acquaintances in his house on a feast-day in honor of the Thracian goddess, Bendis (the Greek mythological goddess Artemis, goddess of the moon). Some of the guests simply audit the debate and remain silent; some are very minor participants in the dialogue. The main speakers are Socrates (the persona for Plato, as in all the dialogues); Cephalus; Polemarchus, Cephalus' son; Thrasymachus, a teacher of argument, a Sophist; and Glaucon and Adeimantus, Plato's elder brothers. (Mr. Scott Buchanan, whose suggested etymologies of the names I have adopted, says that Cephalus, Polemarchus, and Thrasymachus show themselves to be caricatures of the three classes in the state developed in Book IV, and that they are more fully developed in Book VIII.)

A Brief Synopsis

The major intent of the debate in the *Republic* is to determine an extended definition of what constitutes Justice in a given state, whether or not a concept of Justice may be determined by citizens in a given state at the time that Plato is writing, and how Justice may be *accomplished* in a given state (how laws might be enacted that would serve the citizens of a just state in courts of law). Thus it is that the conversation in the *Republic* proceeds from a question of *meaning* (what *is* Justice?), augmented by questions of *fact* (are there *examples* of justice in action or of just men?), to a question of *policy* (what laws may be effected to ensure the carriage of justice?). Of course if a given state could be founded on a resolution and emulation of such precepts, it would be an ideal state; Plato is generally acknowledged to be an idealistic philosopher.

The argument advanced in this dialogue, then, is an attempt to outline a possible and realistic policy for securing well-being and happy concord (the good life) for the citizens of the state: *just* citizens dwelling in a *just* state. The *Republic*, we are reminded, is translated from a dialogue first written in ancient Greek; perhaps a better translation of its title might be the *State*, or the *Ideal State*.

As Plato advances the argument in this dialogue, he sees that he will have to incorporate questions having to do with the education of the ideal citizens; questions having to do with the place of the fictive arts (music, poetry, drama, and so on) in his ideal state, and the philosophies and metaphysics (true knowledge) from which these things ensue.

List of Speakers

Socrates   The major speaker in the dialogue. His name means "master of life," and it is he who advances all of Plato's theories. Note that the Socrates who speaks in Plato's *Dialogues* is not, of course, the man, Socrates. The Socrates of the *Dialogues* serves as a *persona* (a mask, or fictive character) for Plato himself, who hoped, perhaps, thus to grant a kind of immortality to his teacher.

Cephalus   A wealthy and retired old businessman, head of a business family. Socrates has known him a long time and admires him. Cephalus and Socrates initiate the dialogue, which begins with a casual friendly conversation. Cephalus' significance in the dialogue is that he exemplifies the seasoned *experienced* man who, though not a philosopher, has tried to live the good life and to adopt the virtues he has heard about. His remarks to Socrates at the beginning of the dialogue foreshadow topics that Socrates will develop later in the dialogue.

Polemarchus   Cephalus' son and the pupil of Lysias, a teacher of rhetoric. It is Polemarchus (whose name means "war-lord" or "general") who instigates the flyting with Socrates during the festivities for the goddess Bendis before the dialogue proper begins. Polemarchus, perhaps true to his name, is very laconic in the dialogue, and he seems impatient with his "role" in it, seems resigned to his having "inherited" the responsibilities of host after Cephalus quits the conversation.

Thrasymachus   A sophist, a teacher of specious rhetoric. His name means "rash fighter." Socrates seems particularly eager to engage Thrasymachus' arguments in the dialogue, and the two nearly reduce a philosophical dialogue to a petty quarrel.

Adeimantus   An older half-brother of Plato. His name means "sooth-singer," and in the dialogue, he is a young man and something of a poet.

Glaucon   Also a half-brother of Plato. His name means "owl" or "gleaming eyes," and in the dialogue, he is a young man.

CRITICAL COMMENTARIES

Book I
Section One

Summary

The dialogue begins with what is apparently a friendly and innocuous conversation between Socrates and Cephalus, in which Socrates asks Cephalus what he has learned from having lived a long life during which Cephalus has managed to acquire a certain amount of money. Socrates asks Cephalus whether age and the *experience* of age have taught him anything, whether he misses the sexual appetites of his younger years, and whether the accrual of wealth may be said to be a good thing or a bad thing. Cephalus replies that he is happy to have escaped his youthful sexual appetite (one of many passions he has learned to overcome), that wealth in age provides a man the liberty of always telling the truth (never misrepresenting himself in word or deed), and that one obvious advantage of money is that it enables a man to pay his just debts. Thus it is, says Cephalus, that a man may achieve the good life and achieve justice.

Socrates then concludes that justice may be defined as telling the truth and paying one's debts. But, he says, what if a friend in a reasonable state of mind were to lend you a sword or a knife and later, in a crazed state, should ask for the repayment of the debt? Ought one to remind a friend who is in a crazed state that he is mad, and ought one to return a sword to a crazy person? The answer is plain: No.

Socrates concludes that telling the truth and paying one's debts is not necessarily always just. It is at this point that Cephalus excuses himself from the conversation.

Commentary

Socrates' brief conversation with Cephalus is only apparently innocuous; this exchange actually foreshadows several aspects of the just life and the establishment of the just state that will be attempted in the duration of the argument for the *Republic*.

Character Insight

During Plato's time, Greek thinkers had already established the idea that the good man possesses four cardinal virtues: *courage, temperance, justice*, and *wisdom*. In Cephalus, Socrates seems to have met a man who, through the experience of age, seems to have achieved the virtue of *courage* in that one's denial of the passions (one of which is boundless sexual appetite) requires a kind of courage perhaps surpassing physical courage in combat; in learning to temper his passions, he has achieved *temperance*. At the same time, Cephalus seems to have attempted to achieve *justice* in that he tells the truth and repays his debts, and he has tried to think his way through to achieving right conduct and, perhaps, the good life. But as soon as it becomes clear that Socrates has an intricate philosophical subject in mind (the attainment of justice and the establishment of justice for all), Cephalus excuses himself from the conversation: It is plain that he does not pretend to be a philosopher (to love knowledge for its own sake), and, having achieved knowledge, to have achieved wisdom.

Socrates has made it plain in the dialogue that we have not achieved justice because we have not even been able to define justice. Cephalus, in retiring from the conversation in order to sacrifice to the goddess, may be said to be rendering a *kind* of justice to the gods. But in the dialogue, it is clear that we cannot have achieved justice because we have not thus far been able even to *define* justice.

Glossary

the Piraeus   Athens' port on the Saronic Gulf of the Aegean Sea; now a city, Piraeus (or Peiraeus).

Thracians   natives of the ancient country of Thrace (or Thracia) on the Balkan peninsula, which extended to the Danube.

"the goddess"   i.e., Bendis, the Thracian Artemis (the goddess of the moon, wild animals, and hunting, in classical Greek mythology; identified with the Roman goddess Diana).

Sophocles   (496?–406 B.C.) Greek writer of tragic dramas.

Pindar   (522?–438? B.C.) Greek lyric poet.

Simonides   (556?–468? B.C.) Greek lyric poet.

Book I
Section Two

Summary

Upon Cephalus' excusing himself from the conversation, Socrates funnily remarks that, since Polemarchus stands to inherit Cephalus' money, it follows logically that he has inherited the debate: What constitutes justice and how may it be defined?

Polemarchus essentially recapitulates his father's remarks in the previous friendly conversation: Justice, he says, is exemplified in "giving everyone what is due and proper to him." But Socrates is adamant in his refusal of the validity of such a definition, and he returns to his analogy of the friend and the sword. Surely, he says, this cannot be said to constitute justice.

Polemarchus agrees and then argues that justice may be defined as giving everyone what is "appropriate" to him and that it would be unjust to return a sword to a friend who is in a crazed condition. Then Polemarchus argues that it *is* appropriate to do good for one's friends and to do harm to one's enemies, and thus is justice attained.

But Socrates refuses this definition, too: By a series of analogies, he tries to illuminate the argument by showing that many classes of men engaged in various occupations might be said to be better, in given conditions, at doing good for friends and at harming enemies; in other words, there may be said to be infinite ways of accomplishing a "good" or a "bad," but all of these instances argued cannot be said to exemplify the accomplishment of *justice*. It is not the *just* man who is in any given instance best able to accomplish a given benefit or a harm. Justice, in fact, appears in these instances to be of no value.

And, Socrates continues, it is a given that the possibility exists that our friends may be in fact bad, or unjust, men; and it can be that our enemies may be good men, no matter the reason that we have incurred their enmity. Thus it is that, according to Polemarchus' definition of justice, in our ignorance we may do good to bad men and harm to good men, and surely this is not the achievement of justice.

And so Polemarchus agrees to another re-definition: Justice may be defined as doing good for friends who are *in fact* good men and in punishing those who are *in fact* bad men.

But again, Socrates demurs: He argues that returning evil for evil does not constitute justice. Analogically, he argues that if we harm a horse, we make that horse a worse horse; if we harm a dog, we simply achieve a worse dog. If we agree that a good man is a just man, then a worse (unjust) man cannot be said to have been made better if we do evil to him; such a course would only serve to make him more unjust. Thus Socrates argues that we cannot achieve justice by doing evil to men who are already evil, and unjust. And Polemarchus concurs with this conclusion.

Commentary

Literary Device

As the argument grows more complex, so do the methods of argument in the dialogue grow more intricate. In arguing things apparently far removed from the point of the argument (justice, the just man), Socrates is attempting to elucidate the point of the argument by arguing similar instances; that is, he is arguing *analogies*. Socrates descries a single *like* aspect in the series of analogies he argues: a horse, a dog, a horseman, a musician—all may be said individually to possess a distinct *essence* or *virtue* or *quality*. Thus if we do injury to a given thing's essence, we may be said to do injury to the virtue of a given thing or being. We have agreed that the virtue of a human being is justice, or his sense of justice. It follows, then, that if we do evil to another human being, we are perpetuating an injustice; we cannot achieve justice by committing unjust acts.

As we have said, Socrates is citing analogies in his argument in order to clarify the point of the debate; analogies are permitted in argument if they do in fact clarify the point of the debate. Analogies *cannot* be used as proof; and we must always determine the worth of a given analogy by demonstrating its similarities to the point of a given argument. If the analogy is shown to be similar in significant aspects to the point of the argument, it is said to be a valid analogy. If the analogy is determined to be entirely dissimilar, it is a false analogy and may be dismissed from the argument.

As Socrates argues his series of analogies, he is trying to establish argumentative premises; he is citing particular instances in order to establish a general valid premise (a universal truth, sometimes called a *categorical assertion*). If he (or any thinker) can establish a categorical assertion, then he may proceed to deduce truths about particular instances of a given category. The premise that Socrates seeks to establish is a workable definition of justice, the just man.

Thus far in the dialogue, we have been unable to arrive at a conclusion of what justice is, but we have determined several instances of what it is *not*. This is useful: Argumentatively we may determine what a given thing is by determining, through a process of elimination, what it is *not*.

Glossary

draughts   a board game like checkers.

Homer   semilegendary Greek epic poet of the eighth century B.C.: the *Iliad* and the *Odyssey* are both attributed to him.

Odysseus   the hero of the *Odyssey*, a king of Ithaca and one of the Greek leaders in the Trojan War: Latin name *Ulysses*.

Book I
Section Three

Summary

Polemarchus seems to accept Socrates' argument, but at this point, Thrasymachus jumps into the conversation. He objects to the manner in which the argument is proceeding. He regards Socrates' questions as being tedious, and he says, professional teacher of argument that he is, that it is time to stop asking questions and to provide some answers. But Socrates says that he knows that he does not know, at this point, what justice is. What, he says, is Thrasymachus' definition of justice?

Thrasymachus says that he will provide the answer if he is provided his fee. He then says that justice is whatever is in the interest of the stronger party in a given state; justice is thus effected through power by people in power. People in power make laws; the weaker party (subjects) are supposed to obey the laws, and that is justice: obedience to laws made by the rulers in the interest of the rulers.

Socrates then argues that rulers can pass bad laws, "bad" in the sense that they do not serve the interest of the rulers. Thrasymachus says that a ruler cannot make mistakes. Thrasymachus' argument is that might makes right.

But Socrates rebuts this argument by demonstrating that, as a ruler, the ruler's chief interest ought to be the interests of his subjects, just as a physician's interest ought to be the welfare of his patient. A doctor may receive a fee for his work, but that means simply that he is also a wage-earner. A ruler may also receive a living wage for his work, but his main purpose is to rule.

Commentary

Thrasymachus is a professional rhetorician; he teaches the art of persuasion. Furthermore, he is a *Sophist* (he teaches, for a fee, men to win arguments, whether or not the methods employed be valid or logical or to the point of the argument). The ancient Greeks seem to have distrusted the Sophists for their teaching dishonest and specious methods of winning arguments at any cost, and in this dialogue, Thrasymachus seems to exemplify the very sophistry he embraces.

Literary Device

It is clear, from the outset of their conversation, that Socrates and Thrasymachus share a mutual dislike for one another and that the dialogue is likely at any time to degenerate into a petty quarrel. Both speakers employ verbal irony upon one another (they say the opposite of what they mean); both men occasionally smilingly insult one another. At one point, Thrasymachus employs an epithet (he calls Socrates a fool); Thrasymachus in another instance uses a rhetorical question meant to demean Socrates, asking him whether he has a bad nurse who permits Socrates to go sniveling through serious arguments.

Style & Language

Thrasymachus opens his whole argument by pretending to be indignant at Socrates' rhetorical questions he has asked of Polemarchus (Socrates' series of analogies). Socrates, no innocent to rhetoric and the ploys of Sophists, pretends to be frightened after Thrasymachus attacks by pretending to be indignant. So Thrasymachus acts like he is infuriated, for effect, and Socrates acts like he is frightened—for effect. When Socrates validly points out that Thrasymachus has contradicted himself regarding a ruler's fallibility, Thrasymachus, using an epithet, says that Socrates argues like an informer (a spy who talks out of both sides of his mouth). The point of this is that none of it advances the logical or well-reasoned course of the discussion.

Character Insight

For the Greeks, Thrasymachus would seem to lack the virtues of the good man; he appears to be a bad man arguing, and he seems to want to advance his argument by force of verbiage (loud-mouthery) rather than by logic. He is intemperate (out of control); he lacks courage (he will flee the debate); he is blind to justice as an ideal; he makes no distinction between truth and lies; he therefore cannot attain wisdom. Both Cleitophon (hitherto silent) and Polemarchus point out that Thrasymachus contradicts himself at certain stages of the debate. The Greeks would say that Thrasymachus devoids himself of virtue because he is so arrogant (he suffers from *hubris*); he is a power-seeker who applauds the application of power over other citizens. People like him, we are reminded, murdered the historical Socrates; they killed him in order to silence him. Plato knows this.

But whatever his intent in the discussion, Thrasymachus has shifted the debate from the definition of justice and the just man to a definition of the ruler of a state. And Thrasymachus seems to applaud the devices of a tyrant, a despot (a ruler who exercises absolute power over people), no matter whether or not the tyrant achieves justice for his subjects.

At this juncture in the dialogue, Plato anticipates an important point to be considered at length later in the debate: What ought to be the characteristics of a ruler of state?

Glossary

Xerxes (519?–465 B.C.); king of Persia (486–465): son of Darius I. Here, Xerxes, Bias, and Perdiccas are named as exemplars of very wealthy men.

Theban a native of Thebes (ancient city in southern Egypt, on the Nile, on the site of modern Luxor and Karnak).

Polydamus the name of a contemporary athlete, a pancratiast (see next entry).

pancratiast a participant in the *pancratium*, an ancient Greek athletic contest combining boxing and wrestling.

tyrannies plural of *tyranny*, a form of government in which absolute power is vested in a single ruler; this was a common form of government among Greek city-states and did not necessarily have the pejorative connotation it has today, although (as shall be seen) Plato regarded it as the worst kind of government.

democracies plural of *democracy*, a government in which the people hold the ruling power; democracies in Plato's experience were governments in which the citizens exercised power *directly* rather than through elected representatives.

aristocracies plural of *aristocracy*, a government by the best, or by a small, privileged class.

Book I
Section Four

Summary

Thrasymachus continues to bluster and to engage in *persiflage* (whistle-talk). He argues that most people are "good" in appearance only; they do "right" things or try to pursue *dike* (the way things ought to be) only because they are ignorant, or stupid, or afraid of the punishment of the law. Strong men and intelligent men have the courage to do wrong; they can out-think simpler citizens and overpower weaker ones, weaker in whatever sense. Injustice (*adikia*) is the best course of action; the unjust man can take advantage of his fellows in every instance; he can cheat on his taxes, rob the public coffers and defraud the public, juggle books in a position of trust, and so on. And if one steals, Thrasymachus says, one ought to steal big. The more power, the better: The tyrant's life is the good life. At this point, Thrasymachus would like to leave the debate.

Socrates says that Thrasymachus is wrong on three counts: that the unjust man is more knowledgeable than the just, that injustice is a source of strength; and that injustice brings happiness.

In his argument at this point, Socrates again employs analogies, in this case the physician and the flute-player. We notice, Socrates says, that it is the ignorant man who always attempts home-remedies; always the man ignorant of music who attempts to outdo the musician and thereby shows his ignorance of the art.

Next, Socrates reminds Thrasymachus that even thieves have to trust one another and to show it by a fair division of their ill-gotten gain. That is, they too have to practice a kind of justice; otherwise, a gang of thieves would break up and their little "state" would degenerate into disunity, chaos, unhappiness. Unjust men, at whatever level of their practicing injustice, degenerate from an assumed strength to weakness.

Socrates' next argument advances analogies of the pruning hook, the eye, the ear, and the soul, all of which possess their several essences, what we may call their essential functions, or virtues. The eye sees, the ear hears, the pruning knife cuts well. These are their several virtues. What of man and his virtue in this instance? Man's virtue herein is his justice; it enables him to live well in harmony with others and to be happy. Only justice can bring happiness. Injustice at whatever level brings chaos, discord, unhappiness. In thus producing happiness, justice may be said to be more profitable than injustice.

At this point Thrasymachus quits the debate.

Commentary

Beginning with his theory that might makes right, Thrasymachus is now advocating that injustice is better than justice; injustice is better for the individual. Thrasymachus is arguing that crime pays. Thrasymachus herein is arguing a kind of situational ethics; he is praising the benefits of amorality, and he here attempts to stand the entire argument on its head.

At the same time, we may find fault with Socrates' argument from analogy. Socrates is arguing that a man who prescribes medicine for himself has a fool for a physician, but we might object that a given man's ignorance in this instance may be said to be inconclusive; much the same is true of the flute-player analogy. The comparisons attempted here may not agree in sufficient points.

Socrates then argues that it follows that there must be a kind of honor among criminals, that in order to retain some sort of communal strength, they must practice a kind of honor. But Thrasymachus seems to have been arguing for man as an *isolato*, a self-sustained creature who does not require any sense of community.

Socrates' third rebuttal is also rather vague; the analogies he seeks to advance are not very clear, and it is difficult to perceive their essential similarities as being readily similar to the essence of the good man and his pursuit of justice.

Plato is probably not attempting to argue conclusively at this point; he has at this juncture in the *Republic* noticed that he is going to be required to extend his definition, argue more examples, adopt further analogies in order to amplify his argument and bring it to a close. As many readers and students over the centuries have remarked, Book I of the *Republic* may be viewed as an introduction to the conversation in its entirety.

So we are left more or less in the dark in our ideas of "the good life" and "happiness" and "justice" thus far in the proceedings. For Thrasymachus, these concepts seem to come to fruition in a power-grab motivated by simple greed. For Socrates, the attainment of these things seems to involve a deeper philosophical impact (ethical, perhaps spiritual choices).

And we have not yet defined "justice."

Glossary

lyre   a small stringed instrument of the harp family, used by the ancient Greeks to accompany singers and reciters.

end   i.e., purpose, the object for the sake of which a thing exists or is made.

epicure   a person who is especially fond of luxury and sensual pleasure; especially (and here), one with sensitive and discriminating tastes in food or wine. (The English word *epicure* is derived from the name of third-century B.C. Greek philosopher Epicurus; thus its use in translations of Plato is anachronistic.)

Book II
Section One

Summary

Thrasymachus is now out of the dialogue, having gracelessly told Socrates that Socrates was all along seeking to do Thrasymachus personal injury in making him look bad in the argument and that Socrates probably cheated somehow in achieving the final rebuttal. But Glaucon and Adeimantus want the conversation extended, Glaucon because he would like to accept Socrates' argument that justice is better than injustice, but he is not yet convinced; Adeimantus because he is troubled by the efficacy of the *appearance* of virtue as opposed to the *possession* of virtue in and of itself. Adeimantus is also troubled by other aspects he wants introduced in the dialogue. In other words, Glaucon wishes to hear Socrates amplify his rebuttal of Thrasymachus, so Glaucon will recapitulate Thrasymachus' arguments. And Adeimantus intends to break new ground in the conversation.

Socrates has said that Justice is a good, a virtue, not unlike good health and forms of human knowledge that are good in and of themselves. The attainment of the good is not consequent on the rewards (money, honor, prestige) it might entail.

But Glaucon's recapitulation of Thrasymachus' argument is of value, if only because it eschews the Sophist's bombast. Here it follows:

In the old days, there was no concept of justice, no laws to fix the locus of justice. People took by force of arms whatever they could from one another, but no group of people could ally themselves in sufficient force or philosophical consensus to assure their position of power. So they were unhappy because everyone was effecting retribution of evil upon others who had instigated the use of force, violence for violence, blood feuds, the wrongs of fathers visited upon sons. So people agreed to a sort of rude law, tried to establish "right" actions and "wrong" actions. But their laws were engendered by fear and motivated by selfish ends.

Let us suppose (Glaucon continues) that each of two men possesses a magic ring that enables each man to become invisible. One of these men is a just man; the other is unjust. The men's invisibility-at-will enables them to do whatever they want, take whatever they want, seize any opportunity at will. And given the opportunity, both men would seize it and exploit it; the unjust man will behave unjustly; the just man, given the opportunity, will also behave unjustly unless he is a simpleton. Furthermore, Socrates has argued that justice is a virtue, that it is better in and of itself than injustice, no matter the circumstances. No, says Glaucon, it is more rewarding for the unjust man, reaping the benefits of injustice, to *appear* to be just, thereby incurring honors and reputation consequent upon the *appearance* of justice.

Moreover, Adeimantus chimes in with his brother, in attempting to fix a definition of justice, we have been talking about the ideal. In mundane reality, when fathers and teachers advise sons and students to strive for justice, they are actually advising the *appearance* of justice. So Glaucon is correct, and Thrasymachus, in spite of his specious rhetoric, is probably correct. And even if we are reminded that we are taught that the gods themselves reward justice and punish injustice, we know from the stories the poets tell us that the gods can be bribed. Perhaps we can fool the gods with *appearance* as well as the most of mankind. So in order for Socrates to demonstrate that justice is finally good in and of itself, and injustice commensurately bad, we need a furtherance of that argument.

Commentary

Glaucon and Adeimantus have refined Thrasymachus' argument and have augmented it. Now they want a more profound argument proving that, infinitely, justice *qua* justice is preferable to injustice *as* injustice. Furthermore, the two older brothers want Socrates to eschew any discussion of *reputation* of justice in his answer; for it has already been established that mankind generally mistakes the *appearance* of justice for justice. The ideally unjust man is no simpleton, and he becomes adept at concealing his injustice under the guise of justice; no matter how hard he has to work at it, the rewards are great, and he is doubly rewarded in that he can enjoy the fruits of his injustice and at the same time he can enjoy the reputation of being a just man. Thus it is that appearance is all, and, to coin a phrase, the unjust man hereby profits both from the injustice and the appearance of justice, thereby selling his fellows both a doughnut and the hole in the doughnut. And, even if a truly unjust man perceives himself to be a hypocrite, he is finally a happy hypocrite. Besides, it is common knowledge that the hypocrite is recognized as such only by himself and by the gods. Further, it is common knowledge that the gods can be propitiated by sacrifice, so it follows that the clever unjust man may go merrily through life, alternately sinning and sacrificing to the gods, enjoying the best of both worlds. *And,* if we strip the just man of his reputation and honors for being just, then he finally stands naked in his simplicity: He is a just man, but only that.

So we return to the concepts of opportunity and necessity. If the unjust man perceives himself to be in a situation whereby he may profit, he may and will choose either just or unjust measures to ensure that profit. After all, if we are talking of the truly unjust man, then finally he does not even care for the *appearance* of being just. Like most of us, the unjust man has heard the poets tell stories of just men who are thought to be unjust, and those just men are in the myths forced to undergo all sorts of tortures before they are finally executed. So according to the myths, perhaps both the gods and men are united in "making the life of the unjust better than the life of the just." This being the case, if either the just or the unjust man finds himself between two crowds shouting, he had better shout with the louder; if the just man finds himself driven by necessity and want in this world, he had better assuage that want by whatever means necessary, unless he is a simpleton. So the question remains: What is the value of justice?

In their defense of Thrasymachus' arguments, both Glaucon and Adeimantus are *adducing* new evidence into the discussion, and they are both, echoing Thrasymachus, arguing a *situational ethic*. If they could argue from universal truths, they might elect to argue in *syllogisms*; since they are arguing questions of probability ("if/then" arguments), they are arguing *enthymemes*.

Syllogism:

All men will die. (Universal truth—Major premise)

Socrates is a man. (Minor premise)

Socrates will die. (Conclusion)

Enthymeme:

If that child plays in traffic, he will probably be injured.

Glaucon and Adeimantus want Socrates to present a conclusive definition of the quality of justice. They seek a universal truth. From now on, Socrates will monopolize the conversation.

Glossary

Croesus   (*d.* 546 B.C.) last king of Lydia (560–546), noted for his great wealth. He is often used as an exemplar of great wealth (as in the simile "rich as Croesus").

Lydia   ancient kingdom in western Asia Minor: it flourished in the sixth and seventh centuries B.C.; conquered by Persians and absorbed into Persian Empire (6th century B.C.).

collet   a small metal band used in ring settings.

Aeschylus   (525?–456 B.C.) Greek writer of tragedies.

Hesiod   eighth-century B.C. Greek poet, generally accepted to be the author of the epic *Works and Days*; Hesiod (with Homer) is one of the earliest sources of the Greek myths in written form.

Musaeus   a legendary Greek poet thought to have lived before Homer, believed to be the author of Orphic poems and oracles.

Hades   in Greek mythology, the home of the dead, or the *Underworld*; the traditional belief was that the souls of all who died went to Hades, where they existed as *shades*, with consciousness but mindless and without strength.

slough   a swamp, bog, or marsh, especially one that is part of an inlet or backwater.

"mendicant prophets"   prophets or holy men who live by begging; Socrates' implication here is that they are assumed by educated persons to be charlatans.

Orpheus   a legendary musician from Thrace; according to myth, he played the lyre with such artistry that his music moved rocks and trees and calmed wild animals. Orpheus figures in numerous myths and, like Musaeus, is associated with religious rites.

Archilochus   seventh-century B.C. Greek poet, regarded as the inventor of *iambics* (a poetic meter).

rhetoric   the art of using words effectively in speaking or writing; the "professors of rhetoric" to whom Socrates refers here are Sophists, noted for their adroit, subtle, and often specious reasoning.

panegyrists   plural of *panegyrist*, an orator who presented eulogies (praiseful speeches); here, Socrates means writers and speakers who praise, or have praised, justice.

Book II
Section Two

Summary

Socrates begins his reply to the brothers of Plato by attempting to elucidate the argument, and he again employs an analogy. Thus far in the argument, he explains, we seem to have been rather philosophically nearsighted, attempting to find justice in the individual man, rather than seeking it at large in the ideal state. Let us try to read the larger lettering: Let us attempt the construction of the ideal just state.

People unite to form a community because of mutual needs: food, dwelling, the growing of food, and so on. And since it is a given that people are born with various talents, or abilities, it follows that they should be assigned various levels of employment in order to ensure the common good and to perfect the stability of the state: Some should be farmers, some carpenters, tailors, shoemakers, toolmakers, weavers, blacksmiths, manual laborers, and so on. Thus Socrates proposes a division of labor. And we shall require merchants and traders, wholesalers, retailers, salesmen, etc. Thus Socrates proposes a rude balance of trade. Thus the state should be productive and should proceed busily and happily. But where is the justice or virtue of such a state?

Glaucon objects and says that this is merely a well-fed state, fit only for pigs. Reality shows us, he argues, that people seem to require more than necessities; they require certain luxuries, forms of recreation, refinements to life. These refinements are obviously characteristics of a "civilized" state as we know it.

Socrates agrees and provides for these amenities in his discussion. But he notes that by now the small state will have grown and, in the course of its growth, it will begin to encroach upon its neighbors. Such an encroachment historically leads to hostilities: war.

Given this eventuality, we shall require Guardians of the state. History shows us that, no matter how patriotic a given citizenry might be, in arms they are no match for trained soldiers. (Our agreement on a division of labor shows that the various levels of occupation are mutually exclusive). We need real soldiers, professionals, a standing army. We require Guardians of the state.

These soldiers of the state will require careful training. Of course they will have to be more than competent at their tasks, good at what they do, warlike. But in their aggressive and bellicose behaviors, they must know whom to attack; they must never turn against the state. They must be taught to discriminate between enemy and friend, and this involves thinking; thinking leads to knowledge and the appreciation of knowledge, perhaps the love of knowledge. These soldiers must be educated so as to display a certain degree of philosophical attainment. The soldiery must be trained to make intellectual distinctions, must learn to think their way through things.

Commentary

Literary Device

In arguing the merits of the state at large and attempting to adduce from that the merits of the individual, the speaker Socrates is again attempting to employ a manner of systematic thinking, the argument from generalities to particulars (*deductive thinking*). Thus if we can perceive justice in the state, we may be able to perceive justice in the individual. And Socrates in the dialogue continues to employ arguments from analogies.

Character Insight

We must remember at this stage in the conversation that Plato is a child of his times; he is a child of war and various sorts of enmities and strife. Having inherited the genius of his original thought, we must remember to place it in its historical context. Plato did not value much what we might praise as "freedom" or "personal liberty." We have seen that the speaker Socrates has already fixed each citizen in his allotted task in his ideal state in order to accomplish a division of labor and a balance of trade in a smoothly functioning state. Plato thought, apparently, that men could be *happy* at their appointed jobs; in fact, he seems to have distrusted "free spirits," who did not seem to him to accomplish much for the state. Plato, who had lived through the anarchy wrought, in his estimation, from democratic revolutions and counter-revolutions, saw his people as lacking in discipline and purpose in the service of the state. He seems to have thought, in fact, that unlimited liberty too frequently results in mob rule.

Plato now seeks to develop the Guardians as the leaders of the state in his ideal state. Since they are to be leaders, they must be educated in order to develop their philosophical frame of mind.

Glossary

Elegaic   of or relating to a specific verse form, or type of poetry, written in praise of the dead (or, as here, something resembling that type of poetry).

Megara   chief town of ancient Megaris, a district located between the Saronic Gulf and the Gulf of Corinth, site of a battle of the Peloponnesian War.

"'Sons of Ariston'"   i.e., Glaucon and Adeimantus; Ariston was also the father of Plato.

husbandman   farmer.

"plough or mattock"   the plough (or, usually in American English, *plow*) and mattock are basic farm implements for tilling and digging in soil.

neatherd   cowherd.

rhapsodist   in ancient Greece, a person who recited rhapsodies, esp. one who recited epic poems as a profession.

tirewomen   ladies' maids (from *tire*, an obsolete form of *attire* [clothing]).

confectioners   persons whose work or business is making or selling confectionery (sweet edibles, such as candies and cakes).

Book II
Section Three

Summary

We have agreed, says Socrates, that the Guardians must be warlike and fierce in their defense against the enemies of the state. But we do not want them to turn against their fellow citizens. So we may liken their training to that of the family dog, who is trained to befriend his master and the familial circle, but who will courageously attack any threat to the family or, indeed, the neighborhood. So the dog may be said to possess a kind of knowledge; he does not, like a wild dog, attack at random from ignorance (*amathia*). The family dog may be said to be moral in the rude sense.

Thus, Socrates says, the future Guardians of the state must be educated morally; they must be instilled with good morals. We must therefore teach them stories of the heroes and the gods, much as our fathers did for us. But some of these stories must be modified, because Homer and the other poets and storytellers often tell us stories in which the gods commit bad acts, crimes, duplicitous homicides. Since the gods can do no wrong, these old stories must be false and, since children often identify with the figures of fiction, they may be liable to emulate the crimes of the gods as related in these false stories. And, besides, this attribution of crimes and sins and lies and schemes committed by the gods or God is wrong, since it is a given that God is truly good and given wholly to good; thus the attribution of things of evil to God is a lie and the poets who perpetuate such stories are liars.

In other words, whatever evils beset mankind, they are to be attributed to causes other than God, because God is the seat of good things only. And because God is omniscient and omnipotent, God would not be troubled by enemies or plots or the host of things that storytellers have invented. And God, being the fountainhead of all good, is also perfect. God has no need of magic, has no need of shape-shifting or any of that subterfuge that we read about in some stories, in which he might appear as a stranger at the door, and so we are to grant strangers *hospice* (hospitality) because the stranger might be a god in disguise. This is unnecessary and deceitful and, however entertaining it may be, is misleading and might be bad for children who are being trained to be Guardians of the state. Such misleading stories contain crucial lies about God, who is the truth.

Because a man's soul is God *immanent* (God within him), in perpetuating such stories as we frequently do, we allow these stories to do harm to a man's soul, the very essence of his being, and he cannot be led to goodness through portrayals of badness. So we may see that attributing evil acts or thoughts to any form of the god-head is a lie, kind of a mortally generated supreme lie (we do not here mean lies that we may employ against our enemies or lies that we may tell a crazy man in order to placate him, or lies told in the myths of antiquity that we may rewrite to make them serve the truth). The supreme lie is a lie against God; the lying poet has no place in our concept of God. Thus it is that the stories we tell our children must be morally uplifting, and some of the myths are not. Therefore we must winnow the myths, editing them, and, in some cases, censoring aspects of them.

Commentary

We cannot overestimate the importance of the myths of the gods and heroes for the ancient Greeks; this whole body of work comprised for them their nursery rhymes and the entirety of their children's literature. As the Greeks matured, their myths embodied their religion and a great deal of their literary entertainment, and they drew morals from the myths just as later peoples drew morals and draw morals from their reading of scripture in the Bible. This question of the place of morality in literature, and in the arts generally, will be considered as the *Republic* is advanced, and the continued discussion of these questions permeates our own century.

In Plato's time Greek students of metaphysics and theology, and the Greek people generally, had already begun to abandon their *polytheistic* (many gods) ideas and had begun to move towards a *monotheistic* (one god) concept of the deity, or the godhead. This explains Plato's references to the idea(s) of the god-head as "the gods" or "God" as being interchangeable; it clarifies also Plato's making distinctions among the Greek myths (stories) about the gods/God.

The last summary noted the distinctions Plato draws between the stories he regards to be morally uplifting and those that are not. The children of the state, we are reminded, are to be taught only those myths that are morally uplifting; mothers, nurses, teachers are to teach only stories that exhibit a moral impact, and censors of literature are to be appointed by the leaders of the state to ensure that only "good" stories are taught to the children. This idea of the censorship of the arts is continued in Book III. Plato acknowledges that many of the arts exhibit both *figurative* (allegorical) and *literal* meanings, but he argues that young children cannot always make distinctions between things literal and figurative. We must guarantee that the themes advanced in the fictive arts be morally uplifting.

Glossary

gymnastic   physical exercise or education.

Uranus, Cronus (Ouranos, Kronos)   in Greek mythology (told in Hesiod's *Theogony*), Cronus was a Titan who, with his brothers and sisters, was imprisoned in Tartarus (the part of the Underworld where guilty souls are punished) by his father Uranus (the Heavens). Cronos escaped and castrated his father, with the help of his mother Ge (the Earth), to become the ruler of the Titans; this is the "retaliation" Socrates refers to.

mystery   in ancient Greece, a religious ceremony or doctrine revealed only to the initiated.

Hephaestus   in Greek mythology, the god of fire and metalworking, the lame blacksmith god, son of Hera (alone, according to Hesiod; other versions call him the son of Zeus and Hera).

Hera   the queen of heaven and the gods, the sister and wife of Zeus, and goddess of women and marriage.

Zeus   chief deity of the Olympian gods, son of Cronus, brother and husband of Hera.

lots   objects used in deciding a matter by chance.

Pandarus   a character in Homer's *Iliad*: a leader of the Lycians in the Trojan War.

Proteus   a minor sea-god in Greek mythology: he can change his form or appearance at will. In the *Odyssey*, he appears as a seer who changes shape to avoid answering questions.

Thetis   one of the Nereids (sea-goddesses or sea-nymphs) and the mother of Achilles (whose father was a human man, Peleus); Thetis dipped the infant Achilles in the River Styx in order to make him immortal like the gods, but the heel by which she held him was not affected and so became the site of his mortal wound.

Agamemnon   in myth, a son of Atreus and brother of Menelaus; he was king of Mycenae and the leader of the Greek forces in the Trojan War.

Apollo   an Olympian god, son of Zeus, brother of Artemis; he was a god of light, prophecy, healing, music, and archery, and a protector of herds. The shrine at Delphi was sacred to Apollo, and the oracle there was his.

Phoebus   originally a sun-god, *Phoebus* became another name (as here) for Apollo.

Book III
Section One

Summary

Socrates continues: We have agreed, then, that the tales we teach the young will teach them to honor the gods and their parents and to value friendship with one another. Furthermore, we must teach the future Guardians tales that will praise courage and that show fear and cowardice in a bad light. The Guardians certainly must not fear combat; they must not fear death in the service of the state; and they certainly must not be schooled in stories or aspects of stories that might cause them to fear awful sufferings in a life after this mortal life; else they will fear death itself.

Thus we must expunge from the myths all those passages that relate the sufferings of the dead in Hades. We must also expunge any references to the pleasures of drunkenness or any sort of intemperate behavior. However interesting hearing about various sufferings in hell might be, such descriptions might lead to a lack of courage in the face of death, and any sort of exercise in sensuality (like drunkenness) does damage to the function of a Guardian of the state, or any citizen for that matter. So, too, the tales told to maturing young Guardians must extol obedience to commanders and leaders, since it follows logically that honor and obedience to one's parents leads to obedience to future wise leaders, obedience to those more experienced than ourselves being a form of temperance. (Socrates argues a series of examples of stories and parts of stories that ought or ought not to be taught to the future Guardians.)

And, further, Socrates argues that stories which reflect any sort of injustice triumphing over justice, in whatever way, must be expunged from the ideal state. After all, we have not even defined what *Justice* is, so it is unreasonable that we should fabricate tales about it and certainly wrong to teach the theme of injustice conquering justice.

So much, then, for the discussion of the *content* of stories admissible to the ideal state; what of the *forms* the stories may take? Some stories are simple *narratives* (the storyteller tells the story from one point of view), but some stories are *representational*, for example, plays and dramas, in which the characters imitate the speeches and actions of both good and bad men and women; this imitation is said to be *mimesis*. These *mimetic* forms of stories also must be expunged from the state. Our Guardians are to be trained in temperance and to imitate the good at all times, and sometimes we see children copying the bad words and actions they have observed on stage, and it follows that this, too, does no good for the state. Some children who adopt bad roles and role-playing mature into adults who continue to play "bad actors" throughout their lives, whether wittingly or not. Even a pretense of the bad is too close to a lack of virtue itself; besides, however entertaining it may be, it serves no useful function. So dramatic and representational literature ought to be banned from the state.

At this juncture in the conversation, Socrates considers the forms of music, with its aspects of melody, harmony, verse, rhythm, and so on, to which the Guardians might be exposed. These various forms of ancient Greek music, he argues, elicit various emotional reactions from the audience, and some of them may be said to encourage intemperance. Some forms of song, for example, seem to be concerned with the pains of unrequited love; others seem to celebrate the pleasures of drunkenness and to encourage drunkenness. Since these and other examples seem to encourage intemperance, surely they should be banned because they encourage "relaxation" when most of all we require our Guardians to be vigilant. But if there are types of music that are warlike and that encourage endurance in the face of adversity, or are prayerful and function as praise to God in the preservation of the state, they should be retained for their useful function for the state. And, Socrates continues, just as certain harmonies should be banned and others retained, so should the musical instruments that produce them be allowed or disallowed under our superintendence.

So it is, Socrates argues, that the future Guardians of the state will be trained in the beautiful and the good in their childhood, and, as they mature, they will recognize and value these qualities and thus retain their virtue.

Commentary

Theme

Socrates' argument here is essentially that, since children in their innocence may be unable to discriminate between the good and the bad in artistic portrayals of these qualities, there is no good reason to permit children a choice in their formative years insofar as their training in the beauties of "music" is concerned (Plato and the Greeks generally classified literature as a form of music). Permitting the children and maturing young adults a choice in the matter of good and bad in their taste for the arts simply introduces an exercise in liberty that does nothing to advance the cause of the state.

We have in our own time witnessed a continuum of this debate of morality *vis-à-vis* the arts and whether the state is obliged to support artistic enterprises of questionable moral worth.

Glossary

"the world below . . . " i.e., the Underworld, Hades.

"I would rather be a serf . . . " *Odyssey*, IX, 489.

Pluto god of the Underworld, king of Hades.

Tiresias a legendary blind soothsayer of Thebes; much respected, he figures in many mythical stories.

Persephone the daughter of Zeus and Demeter, abducted by Hades (Pluto) to be his wife in the Underworld; she spends half of each year in Hades, half above ground; out of respect for Tiresias' wisdom, she granted that he should retain his mind after death, while the rest of the souls in Hades are merely "flitting shades."

Cocytus the river of wailing, a tributary of the Acheron in Hades.

Styx the river encircling Hades over which Charon ferries the souls of the dead (the third river is *Lethe*).

Achilles the son of the human Peleus and the sea nymph Thetis, and a Greek warrior and leader in the Trojan War; he is the great hero of Homer's *Iliad*. Achilles was angry at Agamemnon as the Trojan War began and required gifts to stop pouting and come out into battle; later he became maddened at the death in battle of his dear friend Patroclus and behaved wildly and dishonorably. These are the actions that Socrates wants the young Guardians to be prevented from reading or hearing.

Priam the last king of Troy, who reigned during the Trojan War; he was the father of Paris, Hector, Troilus, and Cassandra, among the rest of his hundred children by several wives—according to Greek myth.

"Alas my misery! . . ." *Iliad* XVIII, 54; Thetis is lamenting the death of her son Achilles. (This and the quotations and references that follow, up to Cheiron, are illustrative of the kinds of incidents that Socrates believes the young Guardians ought not to be exposed to, because they show the mythical figures and legendary heroes in various kinds of bad light. Many translators, to save space, do not include this section of Book III in their translations. We have taken the list of sources in this series, all but one from the *Iliad* or *Odyssey*, from Scott Buchanan, ed., *The Portable Plato* [Viking], whose edition uses the Benjamin Jowett translation.)

"O heavens! With my eyes . . . ." *Iliad* XXII, 168.

"Woe is me . . . ." *Iliad* XVI, 433.

Patroclus son of Menoetius and the dear friend of Achilles, he is a Greek hero in the *Iliad*.

"Inextinguishable laughter . . . ." *Iliad* I, 599.

"Any of the craftsmen, whether he be priest or physician or carpenter . . . ." *Odyssey* XVII, 383.

Diomede (also Diomedes) one of the great Greek heroes in the Trojan War.

"Friend, sit still and obey my word . . . ." *Iliad* IV, 412.

"The Greeks marched breathing prowess, ... in silent awe of their leaders . . . ." *Odyssey* III, 8; IV, 431.

"O heavy with wine . . . heart of a stag . . . ." *Odyssey* I, 225.

"the wisest of men" i.e., Odysseus.

"When the tables are full . . . into the cups" *Odyssey* IX, 8.

"The saddest of fates . . . ." *Odyssey* XII, 342.

"Without the knowledge of their parents" *Iliad* XIV, 281.

"Ares and Aphrodite . . . ." *Odyssey* VIII, 266.

"He smote his breast . . . ." *Odyssey* XX, 17.

"Gifts persuading gods . . . ." attributed to Hesiod.

Achilles counseled to help the Greeks if they gave him gifts *Iliad* IX, 515.

Achilles unwilling to restore Hector's dead body *Iliad* XXIV, 175.

"Thou has wronged me, O far-darter . . . ." *Iliad* XXII, 15 and following lines.

Achilles' insubordination to the river god *Iliad* XXI, 130, 223 and following lines.

Achilles' offering to the dead Patroclus of his own hair *Iliad* XXIII, 151.

Achilles' dragging of Hector's body round the tomb of Patroclus *Iliad* XXII, 394.

Achilles' slaughter of the captives *Iliad* XXIII, 175.

Cheiron Achilles' teacher.

Peleus a king of the Myrmidons, father of Achilles.

Theseus, son of Poseidon legendary Greek hero, sometimes said to be the son of the sea god Poseidon; he is supposed to have killed the Minotaur and conquered the Amazons, among other feats.

"The kindred of the gods, the relatives of Zeus . . . ." Aeschylus, from *The Niobe*.

Chryses in the *Iliad*, a priest of Apollo and the father of Chryseis, a young woman taken captive by the Greeks; he comes to ransom her, but Agamemnon refuses to give her up, so Apollo sends a pestilence upon the Greek army.

Achaeans in the *Iliad*, the followers of Achilles *or* the entire Greek army; another name for the Greeks. (Historically, the Achaeans were one of the first Hellenic tribes to invade Greece, probably during the third millennium B.C.)

Argos ancient city-state in the northeastern Peloponnesus: It dominated the Peloponnesus from the seventh century B.C. until the rise of Sparta.

tragedy here, a collective term for the plays of tragedians such as Aeschylus, Sophocles, etc.

dithyramb in ancient Greece, an impassioned choric hymn in honor of Dionysus; here it refers to a short poem or chant, usually irregular in meter, with a wild, inspired rhythm.

dicast   in ancient Athens, any of a large group of citizens chosen annually to serve as a court hearing cases; here, an Athenian who performs the function of both judge and juryman at a trial.

Lydian, Ionian, Dorian, Phrygian   ancient Greek musical scales; according to W. J. Baltzell's *A Complete History of Music*, these were all diatonic scales, all like the "natural minor" scales in modern Western music.

"Apollo and his instruments ... Marsyas and his instruments"   In Greek mythology, Marsyas was a satyr (a minor forest god, part man and part goat) who played the flute so well that he entered a contest with Apollo and lost; Apollo, as his prize, was allowed to do whatever he liked to Marsyas so he flayed the satyr alive. (In the following section of the dialogue, Socrates refers to various contemporary theories of music which held that certain kinds of harmony, rhythm, etc., are conducive to certain states of mind, emotions, etc. Socrates wants the future Guardians exposed only to those kinds of music that will prepare them to be courageous in battle; however, he here affects not to know much about the technical details of these musical theories.)

Book III
Section Two

Summary

Socrates turns to a consideration of the physical training for the Guardians, which course in gymnastic should begin quite early in life and continue through life. This physical training, like training in the arts, is intended to teach the Guardians temperance. The Guardians are to abstain from any form of intemperance: gluttony, drunkenness, or any form of sexual license. Thus the training in gymnastic governs diet or any form of physical habit, for intemperance in things physical can result in gluttony, slothfulness, and debility from sexual excess. In fact, intemperance may even result in forms of hypochondria that cause men to invent or develop illnesses that in turn cause them habitually to seek aid from physicians, which would be a sorry plight for Guardians of the state. In fact, the responsible Guardian of the state has an obligation to maintain his good health and not to become a burden to the state. The Guardians are supposed to be too busy to be ill.

Commentary

Theme

Plato sees no real difference in the gymnastic required of children and of professional soldiers; training in the use of arms is simply a difference of degree. The ideal citizen will remain morally and physically fit throughout life. This idea of training in both gymnastic and the academic, a healthy mind in a healthy body, has endured throughout most of the twentieth century, and into the twenty-first, in the Western world.

Glossary

Hellespont another name for the Dardanelles, a strait in northwest Turkey connecting the Sea of Marmara with the Aegean Sea. The ancient Phrygian city of Troy (site of the Trojan War) was located in Asia Minor near the Aegean end of the strait.

Asclepius   in Greek mythology, the god of healing and medicine.

Pandarus   a leader of the Lycians in the Trojan War; a Trojan hero in the *Iliad*.

Menelaus   king of Sparta, Agamemnon's brother, and husband of Helen of Troy, whose abduction by the Trojan Paris (son of King Priam) was the legendary cause of the Trojan War.

Book III
Section Three

Summary

Now, in furthering his concept of the Ideal State, Socrates divides the citizens into three groups: the Guardians are divided into two groups, the rulers and the auxiliaries; the rulers take priority in ruling the state, and the auxiliaries aid them. The third group is essentially the same as has been previously discussed, the craftsmen. As we might expect, the rulers are the very best of the Guardians; they must be older and more experienced men. These rulers must be incorruptible and impervious to bribes; in their youth and as they mature, they will have been tested to ensure their honesty. In other words, the rulers will rule as heads of state; the auxiliaries will police and defend the state; the craftsmen will conduct the necessary day-to-day business of the state.

At this point in the conversation, it occurs to Socrates that the three classes may at some point encroach upon one another and cause discord in the state. What if, for example, any member of a given class asks how he came to be so classified?

Socrates proposes that the citizens be told "just one royal lie," a "needful falsehood." This falsehood is to take the form of a story, the Myth of the Metals, a myth that Socrates discusses in the text. Glaucon is extremely doubtful about the efficacy of this "royal lie" and so is Socrates, but he is hopeful that the myth will ensure the citizens' loyalty to the community and to their respective classes.

Socrates concludes Book III with a few other stipulations having to do with the respective classes. All of these stipulations are intended to ensure the harmony of the state.

Commentary

Theme

By this time, it is plain that Plato's plan for the ideal state has manifested itself, in theory, in a "class society," but, whereas before Socrates has been talking about a division of *labor*, he is now addressing himself to what we may call a division of *power*. Familiar as he was in his lifetime to "power grabs" and revolutions, Plato seems to want to forestall and, it is to be hoped, to prohibit such dissension in the state with the division into three classes and the "necessary lie."

As we have seen thus far, the conversation has presented us with a kind of philosophical mixture of practical statecraft, mythology and its uses, kindred aspects of the arts, and metaphysics. Despite our having agreed earlier that necessary lies may be used to damage an enemy or to placate a crazy friend in distress, we are made uncomfortable by the lie of the Myth of Metals.

We must remember that Plato's is a society in what we may term a kind of "metaphysical flux"; it is a society of a pagan people who, yet quasi-polytheistic in their theological beliefs, seem to be attempting to think their way through to a monotheistic belief. We must remember here that we are dealing with an ancient *Greek* culture; it is not Hebraic. These people have not received the "word" of God; they are strangers to both the Old Testament and the New Testament. In attempting the Myth of Metals, Plato is wishing, perhaps, to ascribe the birth of the children of the three classes to what we may call a prime mover, or a first cause, or the will of God. During Plato's time, his culture was experiencing not only a series of political revolutions; it was undergoing a metaphysical upheaval as well. These aspects of Plato's culture are still warmly debated by scholars of ancient Greece and of the ancient world generally.

In his pursuit of ideal justice and a workable concept of the Good Man, it is frequently said of Plato that he rationalized Jesus Christ into existence three hundred years before the birth of Jesus.

Book IV
Section One

Summary

Because Socrates has now divided the Guardians into two classes (rulers and auxiliaries), Adeimantus says that it occurs to him that the Guardians will not be very happy, in that they will by definition be precluded from material possessions, or the method whereby to procure those material possessions (money). The Guardians, Adeimantus remarks, seem to be more like mercenaries than honored citizens of the state.

Socrates reminds us at this point that the original intent of this aspect of the creation of the ideal state was (and remains) a state where justice might flourish and the *whole* of the citizenry might be happy. Socrates insists that happiness does not consist in the trappings of material wealth; the happy life does not consist, as some might suppose, in a life of revelry and festivity. The happiness of the *state*, Socrates reiterates, consists in the happiness instilled in each individual member of the classes from his having functioned well at his appointed task, performing his job well.

Socrates turns at this juncture to address a specific problem having to do with the craftsmen: They should not be permitted to suffer either from extreme wealth or from extreme poverty. Socrates explains that extreme wealth will cause the craftsmen to become lazy and lax in their duties. They may refuse to work. Extreme poverty will deny them the money whereby to procure the tools of their trade. They may be unable to work. In either case, Socrates argues, such a condition will foment trouble for the state.

Socrates now turns his attention to some other particulars about how the state should be run (the rulers' obligation). Socrates refers specifically to the legislation and the passage of laws. We will not, Socrates says, require many laws in the ideal state; too many communities suffer from an overabundance of too many laws dealing with specific instances (*particularities*), thereby causing us to lose sight of the *generality we seek*: justice for all. The true way to achieve that general truth lies in the program we have already established for the Guardians: education and nurture. This training will ensure a wholeness of vision, that is, the creation of the just citizen in the just state. We ought not to be required to go at the thing piecemeal, floundering in our creation of specific laws and courting a kind of self-defeat. Our Guardians must be trusted to behave in a reasonable fashion. We require only a minimum of laws.

Commentary

Socrates is here recapitulating the argument he employed against Thrasymachus when the Sophist argued that a ruler benefits by seizing all the power and wealth that he can, thereby benefiting himself. No, says Socrates, we have already agreed that the business of the ruler is to benefit the citizenry, and we have agreed that he is a *wage-earner* at one and the same time.

Socrates, in his limiting the laws in the ideal state, seems here to be anticipating a bad state of affairs in which the citizenry spends all of its time neglecting its duties to litigate disputes in courts of law, disputations conducted in many instances by students of sophistry during Plato's own life. *And*, Socrates argues, we have all witnessed those states in which flatterers and hangers-on besiege legislative bodies in an attempt to cajole lawmakers, either through sugared compliments or outright bribery, into making new laws or abrogating ancient laws for the flatterers' gain.

One further point here: Had Plato lived to see the fall of empires other than those of ancient Greece, he would not have been surprised to note that in almost every case, the fall of a given state is signaled by its reliance on hired foreign soldiery (the mercenaries analogy Adeimantus refers to) who abdicate their responsibility to the state in its direst need. For Plato's ideal state, such is not the case with the auxiliaries, native-born and educated citizens who function well and happily in their class, whose material needs are few and provided for by the state.

As we progress in the dialogue, we are ready to seek and fix a definition of the *just* state.

Glossary

"Suppose that we were painting a statue ...." although most of those that survive no longer appear to be painted, the statues of this period, of gods, heroes, etc., were actually painted in various natural colors by the artists.

"The newest song which the singers have ...." *Odyssey* I, 352.

agora the marketplace (literally and, as here, figuratively—meaning commerce in general).

nostrum a medicine prepared by the person selling it; a patent medicine, often sold with exaggerated claims.

"neither drug nor cautery nor spell nor amulet ...." Socrates refers here to various contemporary means of treatment employed by physicians as well as pseudo-physicians: Drugs and cauterization were accepted medical treatment; magical spells and amulets (protective objects, charms) were also commonly used.

cubit an ancient unit of linear measure, about 18–22 inches; originally, the length of the forearm from middle fingertip to elbow. (A man who believed he was four cubits high, in other words, would believe he was about six-foot-six, unusually tall for an ancient Greek.)

hydra the nine-headed serpent slain by Hercules as one of his twelve labors: When any one of its heads is cut off, it is replaced by two others.

Book IV
Section Two

Summary

Having now in theory founded the ideal state, Socrates proceeds to try to determine the essential virtues that may be said to characterize it (the Four Cardinal Virtues): wisdom, courage, temperance, and justice. (See Commentary, Book I, Section One) Socrates first seeks to identify wisdom in the state.

Wisdom in the state must be said to reside in the class of rulers, for, by definition, they rule by counseling the other classes and themselves. They are the best of the Guardians, having all their lives been nurtured and educated to assume their place as rulers, and they are the most experienced and oldest of the citizens. It is they who judge their fellow citizens and themselves. The wisdom of the state is found in their counsels.

The second virtue, courage, may best be found in that class which has specifically been inculcated with courage during the entire career of the members of that class: These are the auxiliaries, who in their capacity as soldiers have become, to reflect Socrates' comparison, "dyed in the wool" carriers of courage. The courage of the state is reflected in their very being.

The third virtue, temperance (discipline) is a bit more difficult of analysis because it seems to permeate the other virtues. Temperance is found in the ordering or controlling (tempering) of certain pleasures or desires in the individual; the temperate man is said to be master of himself. If we extend this to the state, in order for it to regulate itself, we see that the state has to run harmoniously. Every class in the state has to cooperate with the other classes; the classes agree with and actively endorse the functions of all classes in the state. Thus the state may be said to be master of itself, in that the three classes will function smoothly as a *whole* (*the state*) because of concord and harmony among the classes. The class of rulers, wherein the virtue of wisdom in counsel is to be found, agrees to rule in the service of the other classes and of itself; the ruled classes agree to serve and to be ruled wisely. Thus the virtue of temperance in the state is attained.

Having determined three of the four virtues, only the fourth virtue, justice, remains. We recall that the responsibility of each member of each class is that he attend strictly to the business of that class, that each member fulfill the job assigned him. Since we have determined that each citizen is rewarded within the confines of his class by the very virtue of his patriotically performing his class duty, it follows that no other citizen may by force deprive him of the rewards guaranteed him by his class. When we protect a member of a given class by upholding his "rights" as a matter of course, or we protect him by securing his "rights" in the event that someone attempts, by whatever means, to deprive him of his "rights," then we have effected justice and may recognize it as justice in the state.

In Socrates' further instancing the existence of justice in the state, he argues that a choice example of *injustice* would ensue if members of a given class, or classes, should by *force* attempt to seize the "rights" of some other class. However and for whatever cause this forcible violation of class rights might be achieved, if it were to go unreproved, dissension and disharmony would fragment the state. In reproving the evil that is occasioned by the doing of violence to another's rights, justice is attained.

If each member of a given class attends strictly to his own job, and if he recognizes that his rights as a citizen cease when they encroach upon the rights of another citizen, we call this state of affairs a just state.

We may now proceed to demonstrate what it is for a man to be just.

Commentary

Literary Device

As we noticed quite early in our attempt to define what constitutes the dialogue in hand, or any Socratic dialogue, the method of argument adopted is very like that of a debate. It is symptomatic of a person engaged in systematic thought that he or she perceives that the point under discussion is so general that it would be useful to *divide* the point of the discussion into more manageable particulars, the better to arrive at logical conclusions about the point of the discussion. In formal discussions having to do with questions brought before legislative bodies of citizens, this method of seeking knowledge about particulars is known as *dividing the question*, or *dividing the motion* under debate. This is the method Socrates employs in his discussion of the cardinal virtues. In other words, Socrates' method of thinking, here and earlier, is to divide the discussion of the virtues generally and to seek to define each virtue singly. In so doing, Socrates employs a process of elimination: Having discovered and defined three of the four virtues, it follows logically that the fourth virtue is the one remaining.

As observed in the summary, the various classes of the state must agree to be temperate (disciplined) and to live in harmony with one another. This agreement of fixing harmony-in-the-state is one of the earliest examples, if not the earliest, of what is called *Social Contract Theory*; it is the theory advanced by philosophers in the Western world throughout its history. Jean J. Rousseau, in France, advances Plato's theory (*Du Contract Sociale*, 1762), and Plato's theory is reflected in Thomas Jefferson's *Declaration of Independence of the United States of America* (1776). The citizens of Jefferson's ideal state argue, in a very Socratic fashion, that they number among their rights the right of life, liberty, and the pursuit of happiness. For Jefferson's ideal to be realized, his citizens, like Socrates', must agree that their right to their pursuit of happiness must cease when that pursuit begins to encroach upon the rights of others. The perception of this truth is contingent upon the exercise of temperance and justice, as in Socrates' ideal state.

Theme

At this point in the discussion of the ideal state, we should recognize that Plato perceives the state *not* simply as a random collection of human beings; rather, Plato thinks of the state as comprising a sort of being, a kind of entity in and of itself—we may say a kind of organism. The ideal state, comprised of its various parts (classes), *itself* possesses the several virtues we have thus far discussed. And we might anticipate, now, that having divided the ideal state into its several parts (in pursuit of the virtues), Socrates may seek the same division in the individual citizen.

Glossary

smiths   i.e., craftsmen, especially metalworkers.

exordium   the opening part of a formal oration; here, Glaucon refers to Socrates' long explanation about what he is going to say.

Book IV
Section Three

Summary

At this point in the conversation, Socrates seeks agreement that we have attempted to discern the virtues in the state (an argument from the whole) so that we may find the virtues in the individual (argument from the whole to its parts). Socrates says that it would be illogical to presume that the virtues, which stem from some indeterminate aspect of each individual man, are to be inferred from the state. So we were correct originally to seek the virtues in man.

Socrates argues thus: It is a given proposition (a self-evident truth) that a given physical body may not be moving and at rest at the same time. But in the case of a child's toy (a top), we observe that *parts* of the top are in fact moving and parts are in physical fact fixed, or at rest. This is also illustrated in the case of a man whose feet are fixed but whose hands may be waving (in movement). These properties may appear to be opposites, but they are in fact occurring at one and the same time, not unlike the actions of the ruler who rules and who is a wage-earner at the same time.

We may adduce evidence, Socrates says, from the top, the man fixed and waving his arms, and the deductions we may infer from the state, in that the same properties hold for the human mind, or the soul. At times we may desire a given thing and wish to repulse it, at one and the same time. In such a case, our mental state is said to be *ambivalent* (attracted and repulsed, at one and the same time). In such a case, our intellectual stance is said to be *ambiguous* (we are uncertain, troubled). From this, we may deduce that there exist *two* parts of the human mind: reason and desire, or reason and the passions. In order to determine a third part, or element, which corresponds with the third class in the ideal state, may we not sub-divide one of the two we have determined?

At times we may perceive in ourselves a state of mind in which we do desire a given thing, but we are indignant with ourselves for having desired it: Our mental state may be that of self-disgust; we feel self-anger. These various feelings are all human *emotions*, and they exemplify a third element of the mind, or soul.

Thus the essential aspects of the mind follow: (1) reason; (2) emotions or the "spirited" element; and (3) desire, or passions. These aspects of the mind correspond to the three classes of the state: reason, to the rulers; emotions or things spirited, to the auxiliaries; and desire or passions (*concupiscence* is the term Plato adopts) to the craftsmen.

At this point, we discern the four virtues in the individual. In exercising his reason, in which he has been schooled, a man comes to *wisdom*. In exercising his emotions or spirit, in which he has been schooled, a man displays *courage*. In permitting his reason to rule over his emotions and desires, a man displays his *temperance*. What then of *justice*?

Justice may be said to ensue from temperance, a kind of mental harmony, a state in which all elements of his mind are in concord with one another. As in the state, a *tacit* (self-evident) *agreement* must be reached: Reason must be permitted to rule over the emotions and spirited element and permitted to rule over the desires/passions. Thus is justice secured.

Commentary

Style & Language

We must remember that the attempts to ascertain the virtues and to achieve justice have an end in view: the achievement of the good and happy life. In attempting to analyze what we may call the "parts" of or the "particulars" of the mind (or what he calls also the soul), Plato is here interested in pursuing something that he finds to be inherent, or intrinsic, or "born to" every human being. In his use of the terms "mind" and "soul," Plato shows himself to be in the same state of philosophical flux that we noticed earlier in his use of "the gods" and "God." At this stage of his thinking, Plato is unsure of himself; he is, after all, a human being dealing with very intricate philosophical problems.

In his arguing from generalities to particulars, or from particulars to generalities, Plato is seeking to demonstrate philosophical premises and proofs that follow logically. In fact, Plato is attempting to explain *how* he is presenting proofs in his explanation of his use of "relative" terms and "qualifications" of terms just before he discusses the myth of Leontius at the place of execution.

The point is that, hitherto in the conversation, Plato has been presenting causal arguments, arguments that are termed *a posteriori* arguments from proofs presented (literally, arguments which follow; coming behind). In presenting his argument for the inherent verity of the existence of the *soul*, or the *mind*, he seems to want to present arguments *a priori* (fixed and immutable truths which exist *before* we examine them). In short, Plato is attempting an argument for a prime mover, sometimes called philosophically a *primum mobile* (a first cause); this is known slangily as a "God argument." Could it be, he suggests, that God creates the soul, or mind, in individual persons? Could it be that the end of good and just men and women is to educate and nurture the soul in other men and women? This presentation of this aspect of the metaphysical in the *Republic* has engaged the attention of scholars since Plato first presented it.

We also need to consider the significance of mythology in Plato's argument. Plato consistently employs various myths in his adducing evidence, by analogy, in order to argue similarities to the point of his argument. Analogies may be used to clarify the argument; they may not be used as proofs. (They are not examples.) In Leontius' desire to see the dead bodies and his self-aversion at his desire to see them, we perceive his ambivalent feelings. The point here is that Plato so very frequently alludes to myths commonly known to his time in order to clarify his arguments that the *Republic* would be a different book, minus its use of myths. We *know* that Plato is familiarly conversant with the myths that inform his culture.

In ancient Greek myth, Apollo is held to be the god of reason; Dionysus is said to be the god of passions, of desires. In the myth, a well-ordered, or balanced, person is said to be the person who can achieve a balance between the dictates of reason and those of the passions/desires. The Greeks conceived of this by adopting the figure of a balance beam, or scales. Mythically, they agreed that the human being experienced certain necessities, certain appetites for exotic foods, or for intoxicants, or for sexual pleasures, which might be said to be placed on one side of the beam. But at the same time, the story goes, reason must occupy the other side of the beam in order to achieve what they called The Golden Mean, or a middle distance, an equilibrium. This, they thought, resulted in the well-ordered soul and the good life. If there were any question of dominance, things Apollonian (reason) must be permitted to prevail. Reason might admit the necessities of desire and passion; it might recognize also the existence of the emotions. But in the well-ordered life of the soul, reason must prevail over the passions, and the emotions must aid reason in its achieving the state of justice in the individual, thus achieving the good and happy life.

Glossary

Scythians   warlike and nomadic Indo-Iranian people who lived in ancient Scythia, a region of southeastern Europe on the north coast of the Black Sea.

Phoenicians   people from Phoenicia, an ancient region of city-states at the eastern end of the Mediterranean, in the region of present-day Syria and Lebanon.

concupiscent   having strong desire or appetite, especially sexual desire.

Book V
Section One

Summary

Socrates now proposes to argue several examples of injustice in order further to elucidate the concept of justice. Justice is, as an ideal, singular, but examples of injustice abound. As Socrates is about to develop his examples of injustice, Polemarchus and Adeimantus interrupt and ask for a further description of the lives of the Guardians. Earlier in the dialogue, it was determined that, as a part of the social contract, the Guardians were to own everything in common. The question now is, what effect does this have on families and the concept of family in the ideal state? What is to be the status of women and children in the class of Guardians?

Socrates' answer is that, although we agree that women are in the main physically weaker than men, we agreed earlier, in establishing the three classes, that every citizen should be relegated to the job that best suited him. This is true of the women as well as the men, so women should be nurtured and educated the same as men if they are to assume their place as Guardians. Women are to be considered as candidates both as potential rulers and auxiliaries. And their education in the arts and in gymnastic is *not* to be separate but equal: They are to be trained together with the men.

Socrates' plan, in fact, is that the men and women of the Guardian class, being denied all personal possessions, are to share *everything* in common. In the case of this class (*only* this class), the old concept of private homes and family life is to be changed. The Guardians will live together as a single family unit. In order to ensure the highest quality of offspring for this class, the men and women will breed and rear their children in common, according to theories of the eugenic methods employed in breeding domestic animals, such as dogs and horses. Since the Guardians are to share everything in common as members of a new "family," the children will learn to address one another as "brother" and "sister"; they will learn to perceive each older citizen as "father" or "mother," thus ensuring respect and domestic tranquility for this class in the state. Because they belong together as members of a single large family, they should rid themselves of the rivalries and jealousies attendant upon the tradition of erstwhile private "families." This will provide for greater social equality for the members of this class and ought to ensure better unity in the ideal state. *But*, because wives and children are to be held in common, this does not mean that the adult Guardians are permitted to be sexually promiscuous. Their sexual unions must be conducted under strict surveillance by the rulers.

The method whereby this selective breeding will be conducted, Socrates explains, is that at designated calendar times and at the most appropriate periods of their sexual activity and fertility, the men and women of this class will be brought together in "marriage festivals," but they will not be permitted the free choice of sexual partners. Rather, they will be "taught" that the older rulers have drawn all pairs of sexual partners by blind lot, whereas in fact the rulers will have paired the sexual partners by careful selection so as to ensure the success of the eugenic method the rulers have adopted.

As for the children so produced, they will have to be raised communally and provided for by citizens designated as nurses. Furthermore, the children are not to be permitted to recognize their birth parents; the children are not to be permitted to develop "old time" family loyalties; in fact, the birth mothers may be at times prohibited from nursing their children, who will be provided with wet-nurses for their needs.

Glaucon and the other participants in the dialogue are at this point experiencing severe doubts about the efficacy of Socrates' plan; they argue that the plan is too unrealistic, that it will seriously disrupt the order of the state, and that the plan is probably impractical. So Socrates has to answer these objections.

Since *everything* these Guardians now possess is held in communal ownership, there will exist no bickering about private ownership. The old jealousies and squabbles about what is "mine" and what is "yours" and the old ideas about private inheritance will disappear. This has to be seen as the best way to ensure harmony in the state. Since the reasons for internal disorder will have disappeared, this class will function all the more smoothly, because each citizen in the class will feel a common familial bond with every other citizen.

Commentary

Many readers from Plato's time to our own are struck, like Glaucon, by Socrates' proposals at this point; they seem in some instances to be outlandish and almost inhuman. But Socrates' intent, here as elsewhere, is to preserve the unity of his ideal state, no matter the sacrifices entailed in ensuring this aspect of the state. The major objection to Socrates' proposals herein is that these theories, if effected, would in fact depersonalize almost every aspect of the state. Yes, Socrates agrees, that would in fact be the case, and that is what he intends. Personal ambitions, greeds, and petty personal jealousies are the very things that disrupt the state. They breed animosities among and between people. Socrates wants unity and harmony in the state, at whatever cost.

A principal objection to Plato's state-in-becoming, at this point, is that it is communistic. It is. Another principal objection is to the practice of eugenics in the breeding of more select children. This practice is for the welfare of the state; the capricious practice of marriage for "love" or marriage because of mutual "attraction" is unsound if we wish to produce more ideal citizens to serve the state. In Plato's ideal state, *all* sexual intercourse would be more strictly umpired than in any civilized society hitherto.

Glossary

Nemesis in Greek mythology, the personification of the gods' wrath at man's *hubris*; the goddess of retributive justice, or vengeance.

the palaestra in ancient Greece, a public place for exercise in wrestling and athletics. (Athletes trained and performed naked; a little later in the dialogue Socrates will refer to this, comparing the Greeks to other peoples who did not follow the custom [*barbarians*—i.e., non-Hellenes], saying it may have seemed strange when first introduced but was now natural and accepted.)

Cretans Hellenic people from the island of Crete.

Lacedaemonians i.e., Spartans.

Arion's dolphin   Arion was a Greek lyric poet, probably of the seventh century B.C., of legendary fame. Supposedly he was thrown from a ship by a sailor who wished to rob him, but he was permitted to sing one song before he died. He sang so beautifully that a dolphin who heard him was moved to rescue him.

hymeneal songs   wedding songs (after Hymen, the god of marriage).

the Pythian oracle   an older name for the Delphic oracle. (*Pythia* was the title of the high priestess of Apollo's oracle at Delphi; the word is from the same root as *Python*, an enormous mythical serpent slain by Apollo.)

Book V
Section Two

Summary

Socrates now turns his attention to the question as to whether such a class as the Guardians would be *possible*. His answer is yes; we agree that the Guardians must defend the state, and we agree that the men and women and children of this class are to attain equality through nurture and education. Therefore, should violence between two given Greek city-states occur, the men and women Guardians of the ideal state would make war together, stirrup to stirrup, against any enemy of the state. And as part of their children's training as Guardians, they should be taken to war when possible and permitted to witness battles and battle tactics and to witness exhibition of courage and cowardice in the field. And, since they are all so dear to one another (since they are all members of one large family), they will fight valiantly for one another because theirs is a dear cause. But at the same time, after their victories, they must not defile the corpses of their adversaries, must not lay waste to what their adversaries have built up, must not spread rapine and woe throughout the land. If they are involved with another Greek city-state in violently trying to settle some internal discord, all participants are to remember that they *are* fellow-Greeks. After all, fellow-Greeks are not to be treated as barbarians.

At this point, Glaucon and the auditors for the debate again say that the ideas Socrates has presented are probably impracticable. Socrates replies that the intent of the conversation remains, still, to search for a definition of justice *as an ideal*; he argues that a real state, if it could be realized, might very well closely resemble the state he has been theorizing about, but it probably would not be identical to it. And when Socrates is asked what is "wrong" with the real state as we know it, as opposed to the realization of the ideal state, Socrates replies that states nowadays (at the time of the dialogue) have the wrong kinds of rulers.

Socrates then says that civic troubles in the state, in Greece generally, and indeed the world over, will probably never cease, and justice will never be fully realized until philosophers become the rulers or until present rulers and kings show themselves to be philosophers. In other words, philosophy and political power must be melded in order for the ideal state to be realized.

This remark, says Glaucon, is so revolutionary that it might cause more than one important citizen to seize the nearest weapon and attack Socrates. Glaucon demands an explanation of what Socrates has said, so Socrates defines what he means by *philosopher.*

Socrates then recapitulates and develops his analogy of the lover, showing that the lover is a lover, not of the part, but of the whole. So it is for the philosopher, the lover of wisdom and of all knowledge, one who is open-minded and always curious. Glaucon immediately objects; he argues that there exist plenty of people who know things and who display curiosity, but they are surely not philosophers. What about all the followers of Dionysus who flock to any festival site, no matter where; surely they seem to be curious about any new show or spectacle, but surely they are not philosophers. Socrates then defines the philosopher as one who loves the *truth.* At this point, Socrates must present Plato's theory about the nature of *truth and knowledge.*

Socrates, here, adopts Plato's theory of *Forms,* and introduces two faculties of the mind: (1) knowledge of the real and (2) belief in appearances. If, for example, a man can understand the nature of the ideal Forms, then he can be said to understand, through his reason, the true nature of a given Form, for example, *Beauty.* In this case, the philosopher has achieved *knowledge* of Beauty. But if another man sees that some things are beautiful, then, from his point of view, he is said *to possess a belief in the appearance* of Beauty in the thing he perceives to be beautiful. Another example of the distinction (an *intellectual, logical* distinction) that Socrates is making is *Ugliness.* A person who is a philosopher can come to the *knowledge* of ideal Ugliness; a person who sees some things as being ugly *by definition* believes in the *appearance* of Ugliness. The philosopher, the lover of truth, is a *knower* of the truth. The person who, for whatever cause, cannot be a philosopher is one who understands only a *belief* in the appearance of things. For Plato, a Form such as Beauty and a Form such as Ugliness are mutually exclusive; the Forms exist inherently in and of themselves. True Beauty can never be ugly; true Ugliness can never be beautiful. Forms (Beauty and/or Ugliness, for example) are never-changing; they are timeless. Of course some men may disagree about whether a thing is beautiful or ugly, but their disagreement is predicated upon their points of view;

both men are believers in appearance. Again, we are reminded, *the philosopher possesses knowledge of the real; the non-philosopher possesses only belief in appearance.*

Another way of perceiving the distinction between the philosopher and the non-philosopher is to say that the philosopher is wide awake; the non-philosopher lives in a kind of dream world. *Only the philosopher* can understand the Truth and love it as the Truth. This apprehension of Truth involves a knowledge of the Forms, which are singular and ideal, and which do exist; whether or not we are able to perceive them, the Forms are *real*. Men who do not see the reality of a form, such as Beauty, but who call things in the day-to-day world *beautiful* are reacting only to images or reflections of the Forms.

(Another way of trying to understand Plato's theory of Forms is to see Justice as a Form, Goodness as a Form, Happiness as a Form, even Size as a Form. If a man looks at something printed, it appears to be so small that he cannot read it. If he then applies a magnifying glass to it, it appears to be larger, and he can read it. But its Form [Size] has not changed.)

But the whole point of this aspect of the dialogue is to define the philosopher and to defend his credentials as a potential ruler. It is the philosopher who possesses the knowledge of the real; it is he who possesses the knowledge of the Forms as *absolutes*. (Plato is convinced that they are absolutes.) Justice, Goodness, Happiness, the Moral Life—all are absolutes; they may be perceived in their Forms; they are not relative to the times or the changing tides of political favoritism or animosities or "taste" or any sort of the "appearance or belief in appearances." Thus it is that philosophers should be kings. They are best qualified to rule.

As for the Dionysiacs to whom Glaucon referred earlier, and as to current politicians (in Plato's own times), they seem to be passionately involved in their belief in appearances. And their beliefs are always evanescent (fleeting and simply reflective of any given time in the life of mankind). These people are in fact simply amateurs in aesthetics and in statecraft, always followers, never leaders.

Commentary

Plato's word for a given Form may be translated as "ideal" or "pattern"; his word in the Greek is *idea*. But because modern translators and critics conceive of an "idea" as a kind of "thought" which is generated in a given person's "mind," they prefer the term "Form." We must remember that Plato does *not* consider the Forms to be relative; no individual "makes them up" or "conceives" of them. The Forms are absolute and unchanging truths. Justice is a truth.

The Dionysiacs to whom Glaucon refers in the dialogue are in fact theater-goers and devotees of the Dionysian festivals (dramas) presented, for example, in the Temple of Dionysus in Athens. These dramas frequently enact—and adopt actors who suffer from—a passionate *hamartia* (a fatal flaw), a flaw which is frequently *hybris* (overweening pride, arrogance). The themes of many of the dramas result in conflict and eventuate in *adikia* (injustice), and Plato, as we have seen, distrusted the poets who create these dramas and some aspects of the mythologies that inform them. Plato thought that such dramas appealed to the baser instincts in men and that they presented bad examples to the citizenry because their effect tended to unbalance the Greek concept of the Golden Mean.

As the *Republic* continues in its development, Socrates will ban the poets, including Homer, from his ideal state, an act that Socrates has hinted at accomplishing more than once in this dialogue.

One further comment: In discussing the world of perception and alternating misperception of their intellectual attempts to separate knowledge from belief in appearance, Glaucon says that such feeble attempts at reasoning remind him of a children's puzzle, or riddle. Here is the riddle: A man who was not a man thought he saw a bird that was not a bird perched on a bough that was not a bough; the man who was not a man pelted and did not pelt what he thought he saw with a stone that was not a stone. (The man is a eunuch who imperfectly saw a bat perched upon a reed; the eunuch threw a pumice stone [which the Greeks saw as not being a real stone] at the bat, but he missed it.)

Glossary

Ajax one of the bravest of Greek warriors in the *Iliad*; see *Iliad* VII, 321, for the incident Socrates refers to here.

the long chines spines or backbones, or (as here) cuts of meat containing the backbone; what are now called "tenderloins."

"seats of precedent . . . ." *Iliad* VIII, 162.

"They are holy angels . . . ." probably from Hesiod's *Works and Days*, 121 and following lines.

Hellas in ancient times, Greece, including the islands and colonies; the lands populated and ruled by Hellenes.

Dionysiac festivals here, specifically, festivals including dramatic performances. (Dionysus was, among other things, the ancient god of wine and fertility, and his worship often involved orgiastic rites. The evolution of tragedy is linked to Dionysiac worship, and the performance of tragedies was part of yearly festivals in honor of the god.)

Book VI
Section One

Summary

Having now established the character of the true philosopher, Socrates sets himself to the task of showing why the philosopher would, in the ideal state, be the best ruler. It follows logically that, since he understands the Forms, the philosopher is best fitted to rule; after all, it is he who understands truly the nature of reality. Besides, having come to maturity in his study of the arts and gymnastic, the philosopher will possess the cardinal virtues: wisdom, courage, temperance (discipline), and justice.

Because he knows what Justice and Goodness are, the philosopher would be best qualified to administer justice for the good of the citizens he rules. And because he loves Truth, the philosopher will not lie (he would hate a lie); he will not countenance a lie for his benefit or give tacit agreement to lies. Because his bodily wants and physical necessities are provided for him, the philosopher will not be covetous of material things; he will possess temperance and will conduct himself temperately in the interest of his subjects. The philosopher's whole life's training having been spent in gymnastic and in the pursuit of temperance, the philosopher will possess courage. He will not fear death in the field of battle, nor will he fear death from his political adversaries. For all these reasons, the philosopher will make the best ruler.

Adeimantus objects, saying that Socrates has such *a way of arguing* (his "Socratic method") that any listener must answer in the affirmative to his rhetorical questions. But Adeimantus disagrees with Socrates' *conclusions*. The good philosophers he sees around him, Adeimantus says, are worthless to the society they live in, and the bad philosophers are rogues. But whether because of their general worthlessness or their villainy, the philosophers Adeimantus sees are not fit to rule.

To the surprise of the auditors, Socrates concedes to Adeimantus' statement. But, Socrates continues (at this point he argues a parable of a ship's pilot and his crew), it is the state's own fault that it fails to discern the value of philosophers. In its present condition, no one in the state respects what the philosopher alone possesses: knowledge and wisdom. The present and past politicians in the state as it exists are "successful" simply because they flatter the public as if the public were some "monster" or some "great beast" the politicians can feed to surfeit or cajole through flatteries of various sorts to contain it. We have all seen politicians in the political arena; these politicians have learned nothing except to shout with the loudest crowd; these politicians say one thing and do another. They are duplicitous because they have to be, given the caliber of the society in which they find themselves. So of course such a society, such a public, has no use for a good philosopher.

As for the bad philosophers, the rogues, they have become that way because their society has corrupted them. In a good state, intent on being good, a young developing philosopher might become good and wise. In a bad society, like the one in which this dialogue is taking place, the young philosopher, having become corrupt, becomes subject to the flatteries and ambitions of his fellow citizens, who flatter him in the hopes of *realizing their* ambitions. In fact, in a bad society, the more intelligent a young philosopher is, the more attractive he becomes to people who want to use him, and the more such people corrupt him. So things go from bad to worse: Because of his public popularity and the flatteries he has accepted, the young philosopher becomes arrogant. Thus the young philosopher will forego philosophy, or he will use some of its attributes for evil purposes. He will become self-seeking and self-congratulatory. *Yes*, some philosophers are bad men, rogues.

At the same time, although good philosophers are useless to a bad state (Plato's view of his society), there may come a day when a good philosopher might become a ruler, which Socrates has advocated in his argument and in its conclusions. Or the day may come when a ruler in political power might become a philosopher. This would be the only case in which we might realize the Ideal State.

Commentary

We might say at this juncture in the dialogue that Socrates' defense of the philosopher-king is simply too idealistic, too reflective of the philosopher, as the historical Socrates is said to have been characterized in the Greek poet Aristophanes' comedy, *The Clouds*. But, were Plato alive today, he might very well reply that our own society is itself corrupt and lacks idealism just as much as his own society did. And at any rate, Plato might continue, have we agreed or not agreed that the philosopher possesses the virtues we have ourselves instilled in him in developing him to be a ruler? A philosopher is more than an "intellectual," a "mere man of words" as Plato said of himself in a letter he wrote to a friend.

This part of the *Republic* is full of topical allusions (Plato is alluding to people with whom he was personally acquainted). At the time in which the *Republic* was written, Athens was a democratic state, a state which showed that it had no use for men like the man Socrates or his younger fellows (men including Plato). And we must not forget that this is the society that executed the man, Socrates, on what we might regard today as specious charges. (See the Life and Background section, earlier.)

In Socrates' qualification of Adeimantus' description of the "rogue" philosophers, Socrates describes the unfortunate career of a young man corrupted by his society and so flattered by his "supporters" that he behaves intemperately and becomes so arrogant that he tries to seduce others to aid him in overthrowing the state. Such a description closely parallels the life of Alcibiades (c. 450–404 B.C.), a vain, arrogant, and enormously wealthy young man who enjoyed the friendship and tutelage of Socrates in Athens. It was young men like Alcibiades who were engaged in anti-democratic activities during the Peloponnesian War. Socrates, as mentioned earlier, was executed for "corrupting the morals" of young men like Alcibiades, whose life of tragic waste and public outlawry drove him to live in exile as an expatriate in Phrygia, where he was murdered in 404 B.C. An example of the typical rogue philosopher, the philosopher "gone bad," may be seen in Thrasymachus' argumentative premises and conclusions (see Book I).

Socrates' concession to Adeimantus at this stage of the dialogue certainly ends on a pessimistic note. There may be, however, hope for the idea of the philosopher-king as the dialogue continues.

Glossary

the god of jealousy Momus, a son of Night; he is also a personification of censure and criticism.

contemn to scorn, to despise, to treat or think of with contempt.

Book VI
Section Two

Summary

Socrates adamantly denies that he can identify a single state at the time of this dialogue that might prove fruitful for the growth of a philosopher-ruler; he says that, because of his environment (the society in which he finds himself), the naturally good, budding philosopher becomes warped. But Socrates anticipates the resultant clamor from a public whom he has accused of being corrupt, and he attempts to placate that public by insisting that a philosopher-ruler would still be the ideal ruler for the ideal state.

The problem, Socrates says, for our producing a philosopher-ruler may lie in the material with which we have to work. We agree that such a ruler must be intelligent, a "quick study," ambitious in things of the mind, diligent. At the same time, the potential ruler must be disciplined, temperate, reliable. But intelligent people may be intemperate and unreliable, and they may lack courage. Reliable people, conversely, are often indolent and bored when facing intellectual tasks; such people are often ignorant and may be stupid. Citizens who possess all the qualities required in a philosopher-ruler will be in a distinct minority.

Thus it is that candidates for the capacity as ruler will have to be more thoroughly educated than we had thought; they will have to pursue a more rigorous intellectual training so that they can attain knowledge of the real.

Glaucon asks Socrates if he means that the potential rulers are to have knowledge of the Forms. Socrates replies that the rulers must possess knowledge of Goodness, for logically that is the sole way a man may recognize the goodness of, say, Justice and Beauty.

Logically, Socrates must at this juncture entertain a definition of Goodness, but we cannot accept the premise that "knowledge of the Good is Goodness"; that constitutes an invalid argument (a false tautology). And some people offer other invalid arguments for Goodness, as we may observe.

Socrates then says that he will not precisely define Goodness, but that he can elucidate the argument by arguing another analogy. Socrates' analogy involves a comparison between *sight* and *knowledge*. In order for men to see, men must be given visible objects to perceive, and men must be given light in order to perceive the objects. The source of this light is the sun. Analogically, in order for men to know anything, men must be able to think, and they must be provided objects of knowledge (the Forms). Visible objects, then, have to be *in the light*; objects of knowledge have to be *true*. Light comes from the sun; truth comes from Goodness. (This analogy has come to be known as the Analogy of the Sun.)

Commentary

At this point, Plato is perhaps alluding to his first trip to Syracuse when he still had hopes of helping his friend, Dion, to persuade the young king, Dionysius II, to become a friend to philosophy and to enlighten his fellow citizens. Thus, in actuality, Plato might have, as he had hoped, produced in Dionysius II an enlightened despot, a king-turned-philosopher. But Plato's plan failed (see the Life and Background section).

Theme

When Socrates is here speaking of Plato's idea of "Goodness," Plato's meaning is "Goodness *itself* "; it is the supreme Form, inherent, time-less, essential; hence, the reflexive, "Goodness *itself.*" Goodness is embodied not only in the cardinal virtues, but also in all of the universe. Earlier for Plato (and for us), Goodness might be achieved through the exercise of the virtues, resulting in the good and happy life (embracing courage, justice, temperance, wisdom). We now are to see Goodness *itself* manifested in the moral universe and in the phys-ical universe (the beauty of the heavenly bodies *and* the order of them). We are to see this supreme Goodness *itself* as a manifestation of a divine Reason at work in the universe. This apprehension of a divine Reason at work permits us to see how the universe works; it leads to our "see-ing" knowledge (the Forms), and the universe is thus illuminated. As illumination, Goodness *itself* is analogous to the sun, which sheds light upon vision and upon things made visible and is the source of all mor-tal life.

Socrates never in this dialogue, nor in any dialogue, defines Good-ness *itself.* But Socrates does say that the knowledge of it may come to one in a kind of revelation after a long course of philosophical study

(Jowett translation 540 A). And we know that Plato says, in the letter he wrote to Dion's friends and family, that he never wrote down a definition for Goodness *itself* (Letter VII 341 c, Harward translation).

We may briefly set forth the Analogy of the Sun thus: For sight, the sun is the source of light, and so makes objects visible and allows the eye to see; for Knowledge, Goodness is the source of Truth, and so makes the Forms intelligible and allows the mind to know.

Glossary

Theages' bridle   scholars identify Socrates' phrase here as referring to a proverb.

the Muse of philosophy   The nine Muses were mythical daughters of Memory, goddesses of the arts, who were said to watch over or inspire the practitioners of nine specific arts: Calliope, epic poetry; Clio, history; Euterpe, the flute; Melpomene, tragedy; Terpsichore, dance; Erato, the lyre (and lyric poetry); Polyhymnia, sacred song; Urania, astronomy; and Thalia, comedy. There was no Muse assigned to philosophy; Socrates is using this phrase figuratively and fancifully, and perhaps implying that philosophy is more deserving of a Muse than some of these other arts.

Book VI
Section Three

Summary

Socrates is still attempting to elucidate his point; Glaucon asks that Socrates continue the analogy. But Socrates introduces a new illustration, *The Analogy of the Divided Line*. Socrates is still making the distinction between *knowledge* and *belief*, the difference between the Forms and ordinary objects. (We should also recall here that Socrates says that objects of belief are like *reflections* of objects of knowledge.) At this juncture of the dialogue, Socrates argues that there exist *two* degrees of knowledge and *two* of belief.

Commentary

Socrates tells us now that there exist *four* levels of what we may call *intellect* (intellectual functioning, cognition) and four levels of *objects that the intellect perceives*. (See the illustration of the Levels of Intellect.)

■   The lowest level of intellect (cognition, thinking process) is called *imagining*. Thinking at this level seems to be the mental activity pursued by people whose state of mind might be called, in comparison to higher states of mind, unclear, or vague. (This state of mind may be manifested in the unreleased people in the *Allegory of the Cave*, which Socrates discusses later in the dialogue. These people in the Cave perceive only images of images.)

■   The next higher level of intellect is called *belief*, or common-sense belief. Mental activity at this level seems to be the thought processes of people who perceive tangible things, real objects, things of material substance. These people, like the young Guardians, hold *moral beliefs*, but they have no *knowledge* of the things in which they believe; they have been *taught* to believe. A higher education is intended for the Guardians as they mature (in order for them to escape from the Cave). The Guardians are to be educated in mathematics and then in moral philosophy.

■ The next higher level of intellect is called *thinking*. Formal training in this level of mental activity involves studying the mathematical sciences. Guardians at this level of mental activity are taught the use of visible diagrams and physical models meant to symbolize the workings of pure thought. Next, the Guardians are taught to reason from assumptions (premises) to conclusions (deductive thought).

■ The highest level of intellect is called *Dialectic*, which for Plato means a conversation (question and response) that seeks to determine, without the aid of diagrams or physical models, a conclusion about some Form, for example, the conversation about Justice in the present dialogue. This level of mental activity does not move from an assumed premise to a conclusion (deductive thinking); rather, the premise itself is analyzed through Dialectic (as in the present dialogue) to try to determine the nature of a given Form. Knowledge of the Form might then be construed as a premise, from which we can deduce conclusions proving out the whole of mathematics and moral philosophy. This level of intellect is also called *intelligence* or *knowledge* (the condition of the prisoner who is released from the Cave in the Allegory of the Cave).

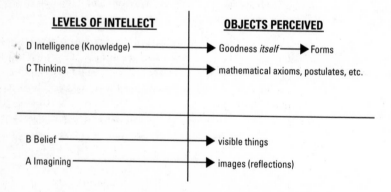

It is important at this juncture in our conversation that we do not confuse Plato's theories on *Dialectic* with the ideas of later thinkers, such as Friedrich Hegel (1770–1831) and Karl Marx (1818–1883), who read Plato and, in their times, advanced their respective theories of systematic philosophy in terms that differ from Plato's.

Book VII
Section One

Summary

Having presented us with the Analogy of the Sun and the Analogy of the Line, Socrates now in the conversation introduces the Allegory of the Cave. Socrates is here still trying to clarify the four levels of intellect, the two levels of belief, and the two levels of knowledge.

For this allegory, we are to imagine an underground Cave, whose entrance/exit leads upward to daylight. There are prisoners in the Cave who have been chained there since their childhood; they are chained to the ground and chained by their heads. They can see only the wall of the Cave in front of them. A fire is burning behind the prisoners; between the fire and the arrested prisoners, there is a walkway where people walk and talk and carry objects. The prisoners perceive only shadows of the people and things passing on the walkway; the prisoners hear echoes of the talk coming from the shadows. The prisoners perceive the shadows and echoes as reality.

If we unchain one of the prisoners and make him turn around, he would be frightened, pained by new physical movement, dazzled by the fire, unable at first to see. When he is told that the people and things he now perceives are more real than the shadows, he will not believe it. He will want to return to his old perceptions of the shadows as reality. When we drag him out of the Cave and into the World of Day, the sun will blind him. But he will gradually see the stars and the moon; he will then be able to see shadows in the daylight thrown by the sun; then he will see objects in the full light of day. The sun makes this new perception possible. If we took the prisoner back into the Cave, into his old world, he would not be able to function well in his old world of shadows.

For the allegory, the Cave corresponds to the realm of belief; the World of Day corresponds to the realm of knowledge. The sun stands for the Form of Goodness *itself*. If the prisoner were to be returned to the Cave, his old fellows would not believe his experiences, since they have always been imprisoned in their world, the Cave.

Thus, allegorically, we must release the prisoners from their Cave: We must give the Guardians the experience of education so that they can become the philosopher-kings of the Ideal State, because they will be able to know the Forms and, finally, Goodness *itself.*

But it is not enough that the prisoner, freed, now possesses knowledge. He must be returned to the Cave to enlighten his erstwhile fellows about the knowledge he now perceives.

Glaucon objects: He argues that for the enlightened prisoner to return to the Cave would make him unhappy. It would be a lot of work to lead his fellows into the light of a kind of new dawn of knowledge. Socrates here reminds us, again, that the business of rulers is not to make themselves happy; their happiness is to be realized in the happiness of every citizen in the Ideal State.

Commentary

It is useful and probably necessary at this juncture that we compare the diagrams of the Divided Line (in the preceding commentary) and the Allegory of the Cave, following.

ALLEGORY OF THE CAVE

	ALLEGORY		INTERPRETATION
World of Day	The sun	Knowledge	Goodness *itself*
	Visible objects		The Forms
	Shadows of visible things		Mathematical models
The Cave	Walkway and fire	Belief	Tangible things, objects of substance
	Shadows on wall		Shadows, reflections, echoes

As the prisoner ascends from the Cave and emerges into the World of Day, allegorically his levels of intellect improve as his ascension progresses. Intellectually, the developing thinker moves from the level of *imagining*, upward to *common-sense belief,* thence to *thinking*, thence to the summit of *Dialectic*, also termed *intelligence* or *knowledge*. (Refer to the conversation about the levels of intellect in the preceding commentary.)

Plato seems to believe that all levels of intellect are somehow *connected*, not disparate; the person who achieves Dialectic has already subsumed the other levels in his progress. For example, the prisoner whom we help ascend from the Cave originally *imagines* that the shadows on the wall are "real things"; when he is permitted to perceive walkway, fire, people, and objects carried, he perceives the shadows as *shadows* of real things. He has learned something "new," but it is a learning predicated upon a previous assumption.

Interestingly, the American philosopher William James (1842–1910) believed that, in the world of ideas, ideas are connected by a kind of next-to-next relationship. James believed that the highest form of intellect is manifested in the ability to perceive similarities in apparently dissimilar things. James called this the ability to "subsume novel data." It is said that, in applying these ideas to the world of "things" and empirical phenomena, James anticipated the science of modern physics. James' theories are interestingly similar to Plato's.

Literary Device

The conversation of the Allegory of the Cave is highly allusive. At that point when we lead our prisoner from the darkness into the light, the prisoner will likely be physically dazed and intellectually perplexed. This condition (perplexity, confusion) is similar to that of Cephalus, who exits our conversation early, and Polemarchus at the very beginning of the present dialogue. Too, Socrates says that, *in order to avoid perplexity*, students should be schooled *first* in mathematics, then in moral philosophy, before they may understand the Good. Socrates suggests, further, that when the prisoner returns to the Cave in order to lead his fellows to the light of understanding, they may be so dismayed at their having been wrenched from their comfortable state of ignorance that they may want to kill him—a likely allusion to the death of Socrates, the historical man. And the allusion is amplified: If the first prisoner, now enlightened by his contemplation of Justice itself, were to be hauled into a courtroom and faced with the unenlightened quibbles of lawyers trained in sophistry, he probably would not be able to defend himself. A character named Callicles, in a different dialogue, derides Socrates with Socrates' inability to defend himself in a court of law (Gorgias 486 A).

We now continue the conversation in order to discover how the Guardians are to be given a higher education.

Glossary

"Better to be the poor servant . . . ."   *Odyssey* IX, 489.

Book VII
Section Two

Summary

In the conversation earlier, it was decided that the future Guardians are to be trained in gymnastic and the arts early in their education and nurture. As they mature, they are to be introduced to various levels of mathematics and thoroughly schooled in them in order to train them *intellectually* so that they may become adept at *abstract thought*. Socrates suggests that the studies should move from the simplest to the most complex in this order: arithmetic, plane geometry, solid geometry, astronomy, and harmonics. We bear in mind that the future Guardians are to be schooled thus in order that they may one day understand the Forms and Goodness *itself*.

Following their rigorous study in mathematics, the future Guardians are to be trained in Dialectic, which field of study has been discussed earlier in the conversation. (Here we should review that summary and commentary having to do with the four levels of intellect, the Analogy of the Line, and the Allegory of the Cave.)

Commentary

Nowadays we regard astronomy and harmonics as belonging to the field of "applied" rather than "pure" mathematics, but this was not the case in Plato's time. "Natural science" as we know it was unknown to the ancients; our practice of observation and experimentation to determine knowledge about phenomena had not yet been introduced. Plato and his contemporaries thought calculation to be more important than observation; Plato himself pokes gentle fun at thinkers he considers to be "star-gazers."

For Plato, the same importance of calculation holds true for the study of harmonics, which Pythagoreans had already advanced. Socrates tells Glaucon point-blank that it is not our intent to teach these future Guardians to keep time, or something like three-part harmony or, so to speak, to tap their feet. We are trying to teach these people how to *think*.

Socrates' allusion to the "shell-toss" preliminary in the children's game may be compared to our "coin-toss" preliminary at the outset of contemporary athletic events.

Glossary

Palamedes   a hero of post-Homeric stories of the Trojan War.

Daedalus   a legendary Athenian inventor, architect, and artist, who according to legend, built the Labyrinth.

Pythagoreans   followers of Pythagoras, a philosopher, astronomer, and mathematician of the sixth century B.C.

"rack [the strings] on the pegs of the instrument . . . ."   Socrates is referring to music theorists who, in trying to determine precise intervals of pitch, tighten and loosen the strings of a lyre to change the pitch ever so slightly; figuratively, he says they are torturing the strings the way a prisoner might be tortured on a rack, stretching them little by little to make them give up information.

plectrum   a thin piece of metal, bone, plastic, etc., used for plucking the strings of a lyre; a pick.

Book VII
Section Three

Summary

We are now presented with the entire program of study for the heads of state in the Ideal State, and we are reminded again that these young candidates must be of high moral character and industry.

Socrates at this juncture in the conversation establishes the program of studies that will govern the lives of the future philosopher-rulers. This program, portions of which Socrates has discussed previously throughout the dialogue, is divided into six parts:

Part 1: From early childhood and until they are about 18, the students will receive their early training in gymnastic and the arts, and they will receive training in elementary mathematics, but the intellectual studies are to be lightly enforced. Socrates argues that rigorous training does not harm the body at this age, but enforced intellectual studies may cause the learner to rebel. And, as previously discussed, the children will ride to battle accompanied by their families so that they may learn warfare and witness courage in action.

Part 2: At this stage, the best of the students will be selected to further their education in a strict regimen of physical and military training (discussed earlier). This physical and military training will be rigorous, and the students will have no time for intellectual pursuits. This stage will last two or three years. (Apparently the students winnowed out at this stage—dismissed, that is, from advanced study—will be given lesser positions in the Ideal State.)

Part 3: After the intensive physical training, when they are 20, the young students will be tested, and a further selection will be made. The best students will be given the advanced studies in mathematics (discussed earlier); the course in mathematics will last for 10 years. The students winnowed out at this stage will form up the second class of the state as auxiliaries.

Part 4: When the students are 30, a further selection is made. (Socrates does not specify what happens to the students who are not selected at this stage.) The students who are selected will study Dialectic for about five years, and care must be taken to show the students that the study of Dialectic is a serious enterprise; it is not a game of wits undertaken for personal grandeur.

Part 5: When they are 35, having now become trained philosophers, the students will receive the practical experience necessary for them to accept their role as leaders of the state. They will take positions in the military and politics and begin teaching their fellow citizens to "see the light," so to speak. This period of service will last 15 years.

Part 6: At the age of 50, the philosopher-rulers will be fully matured. They will now spend the rest of their lives in philosophical contemplation and in ruling and governing the Ideal State. Now that they know Goodness, they will best be prepared to serve the good of the state.

Commentary

Theme

Thus it is that Plato argues that the best rulers must be philosophers. Only philosophers know Goodness; it follows logically that they will act in the best interest of their fellow citizens because, as philosophers, they will have attained *knowledge* at every level.

Glossary

Solon   (640?-559? B.C.) Athenian statesman and lawgiver: framed the democratic laws of Athens.

eristic   of or provoking controversy or given to sophistical argument and specious reasoning; a person who engages in such argument (a Sophist).

Book VIII

Summary

In Book V, Socrates was about to develop his theories of injustice by arguing examples of injustice, when Polemarchus and Adeimantus asked him to continue his conversation about the Guardians. Now (in Book VIII) Socrates returns to his examples of unjust societies and unjust men.

Socrates argues that there are four main types of unjust states: timocracy, oligarchy (plutocracy), democracy, and tyranny (despotism). Socrates says that timocracy is the closest to the Ideal State that we have thus far experienced; the others descend in value as they are listed.

We have already in the conversation discovered a just man and a just state; we shall now determine four types of unjust men corresponding to four unjust states. By determining these types, we shall be able to determine why it is better to be just than unjust.

We are to imagine that our ideal (just) state is slowly decaying and falling into ruin, and that it proceeds from good to bad, worsening as it falls to the worst form of government, despotism. We may begin by examining timocracy and the timocratic man.

Socrates descries government by *timocracy* (from *timé*, honor) in Sparta and in Crete, where the military was in power (*kratos*) and honor and ambition were highly valued.

A given state seems always to fall into ruin because people in power disagree, quarrel among themselves, and come to violence. Theoretically, this situation might come about because a ruler could have made mistaken "marriage matches" at a state-marriage festival, thus producing inferior children with the wrong "mix" of metals flowing through their veins (see the Myth of Metals, discussed in Book III). Some of these children, although inferior, might eventually come to power as rulers, but they would lack the character aptitudes for good rule. These rulers will lack wisdom; they will become ambitious and desirous of money and property; they will prefer the comforts of private lives to the welfare of the state. Their level of intellect will decline; they will value honor and ambition over wisdom. For them, reason will no longer prevail; no matter if they be courageous, they will possess only the intellectual attributes of auxiliaries. Such rulers will be unable to secure justice for the state and its citizenry.

The *timocratic man* will value physical exploits, and he will be courageous and ambitious. When young, he might not care for money, but as he ages, he will become avaricious, and he will be unable to maintain his spiritual balance. He will become unreasonable and no longer in control of himself.

Oligarchy is a society in which the rich are in control; the wealthy are extremely wealthy and the poor quite poverty-stricken. The rich will not be able to sate their desire for more and more wealth; for them the love of money will overtake their desire for honor. The erstwhile timocracy thus declines to oligarchy.

In this oligarchy, the rulers will be chosen for their wealth alone. Money in and of itself does not ensure a good political atmosphere; in fact, in such a state, the gap between the rich and the poor will be so wide that the two classes (rich and poor) will be actively antagonistic to one another. Eventually, the rich will become profligate, simply getting and spending money, in no way of any service to the state; the poor will likely become beggars or criminals, an impediment to the state. Thus we perceive the second kind of unjust state.

We may imagine, Socrates says, a timocratic man, say a great general, who suffers major defeats in battle, so that when he comes home from the war he is deprived of his rights and property and is perhaps driven into exile. His son, *the oligarchic man*, will see what has happened to the father; the son will live in fear of the same thing happening to himself, and his great fear will be that of being penniless. He will have lost his inheritance, so he will have to work arduously for his sustenance, and money will come to dominate him. His existence will probably become miserly; he will not commit impulsive acts, and he may appear to be a reasonable person, but his respectability is predicated upon his fear of becoming impoverished. Such a man is not controlled by his reason or his spirit. The love of money drives him.

Socrates now further rehearses the decline of the ideal state by showing how an oligarchy might degenerate into a *democracy*. The enormously wealthy people in a declining oligarchy will probably lend out money to the poor at exorbitant rates of interest. The debtors will spend and spend; they will be encouraged to borrow and borrow. They will become bankrupt and will see the rich as their mortal enemies, and they will accomplish the violent overthrow of the government and enlist the aid of their impoverished fellows. Thus is an ancient democracy accomplished.

In such a democratic state, everyone is more or less equally free of any responsibility to anyone else, including service to the state. No one is obliged to give orders; no one is obliged to take orders; no justice can be respected or meted out. Rulers will serve at the behest of what Socrates has called the "great beast"; political platforms will become popularity contests. A kind of mob-rule becomes the order of the day.

Although the oligarchic man is able to control himself to the degree that he can maintain an aura of respectability, he is still driven by money, and he will be unable to raise his son, *the democratic man*, well, instilling in him the proper moral values. Although the son may not even respect money, he will probably not respect anything else; he will become shiftless, kind of a reed in the wind, unable to control his desires, which will probably fluctuate wildly. Lacking any ability to discern differences in appetite, he will probably live solely for the moment, and he will be rudderless. His will be a life without order.

If oligarchy is greedy for money, so is democracy greedy for absolute freedom; it recognizes no authority whatever, neither familial nor militaristic nor academic. How does a *tyranny* come about? The erstwhile democrats in power will continue to placate the great beast of the populace, and they will, as is their wont, rob all the rich folk. The rich will complain in the Assembly; the democrats will charge them with being oligarchs and reactionaries. Then the great beast will elect a popular and violent leader to do something, and he will start killing people, and he will become feared and extremely powerful. And he will become fearful, require bodyguards, build a private army, and tax the citizenry to fund his standing army. He will trust no one, certainly not men of reason or compassion. He will surround himself with criminals, and he will finally do criminal acts against the very democrats who elected him. The tyrant will despotically rule his unhappy and fearful state.

The democrat is desirous of all things and treats all, good and bad, equally; if his son, *the tyrannical man*, falls into bad company—and he will—then he will be governed entirely by the bad and the desire for the bad. He will be driven by lust, and his lust will drive him completely out of control. He will eventually become something like a wild beast, his lust will become bestial, and he will do terrible things to get what he wants. No longer able to discern right from wrong, good from bad, he will turn against every man and will earn and deserve every man's hatred and scorn. His life will be miserable.

Commentary

We have now heard Socrates explain the decline of the state and the individual. Of course all of us are familiar with other types of states and individuals and shades of varieties of each. Plato does not mean here that his are the only types, or that each state would necessarily fall in the sequence that he describes; Plato is not guilty here of a *reductive fallacy* (that is, he is not arguing a fallacious either-or argument). Plato sees the conditions Socrates describes as being *symptomatic* of the decline and fall of governments and men. Plato's point is that, once a given state or a given man begins to decline morally, his fall will become somehow inexorable, the plummet to ruin inevitable. Power, Plato would agree, corrupts and absolute power corrupts absolutely.

Moreover, Plato knows what he is talking about: He witnessed it in his own day. He saw the timocracies of Crete and Sparta; he lived through the oligarchy of his beloved Athens; he saw the democrats kill Socrates; he barely escaped the tyranny of Syracuse. Plato was not a stranger to robbers and cutthroats and murderers of various criminal hues. Plato the wrestler and athlete saw the degeneracy of his corpulent fellow-citizens; Plato the thinker did not countenance fools and hypocrites gladly. Indeed, the *Republic* stands today as his fearless rebuke of his own times. His criticism of the states he saw about him is simply that they are ruled by unjust men practicing injustice upon their citizenry.

Plato's hypothetical general dramatized in the timocratic man is quite close to what we know of the Athenian general, Thucydides, who wrote his *History of the Peloponnesian War* as he himself witnessed it. And, had Plato lived to read *The Decline and Fall of the Roman Empire*, or *The Rise and Fall of the Third Reich*, he would not have been surprised at the inexorable direction either tyranny took in visiting its evils upon the citizens of the world.

We are ready now in the conversation to follow the career of the unjust man and to consider why it is better for a man to be just than unjust. We are ready, now, for the major question posed by the *Republic*.

Glossary

magazines   places of storage, as a warehouse, storehouse, or military supply depot.

"made a blind god director of his chorus . . . ."   i.e., avarice; the chorus is a group in Greek drama that speaks for the ordinary citizens of the society, and the Choragos was its "director" or spokesman. Socrates' figure seems to mean that the oligarchic man, having no cultivation, will have allowed this "blind god"—greed or the love of money and possessions—to direct his life and speak for him.

"the country of the lotus-eaters . . . ."   one of the mythical lands Odysseus visited on his voyage home from Troy, the country of the lotus-eaters was populated with people who were drugged and lethargic, lacking in ambition; here, Socrates uses the phrase figuratively to describe the state of being of the democratic man who is a slave to physical appetites and useless, degrading pleasures.

"becomes a water-drinker . . . ."   i.e., stops using alcohol.

anarchy   the complete absence of government; a state without rule of any kind; a chaotic state.

Book IX

Summary

Socrates establishes three arguments to demonstrate that a man who is just lives a happier and better life than an unjust man.

Socrates takes as his first example the tyrant. It might appear to an immature thinker, or a child, that the tyrant, exercising despotism as he does, is surely a happy man; after all, it is plain that the tyrant can live surrounded by pomp and ceremony and all that wealth can buy. All of his subjects he may treat as objects; he can kill any citizen of his state at whim. But we must remember that the tyrant himself is just as much a slave to his own mad master, his lust, as his subjects are enslaved to his tyranny. The best parts of the tyrant's soul are governed, tyrannically, by the worst part of his soul, and he can never escape the dark prison of his days. The tyrant, who is never in control of himself, is miserable.

In contrast to the tyrant, the just man is free; he is enslaved to nothing, for nothing in his desires or emotions can captivate him; since his whole life is governed by his reason, he lives a self-controlled life, happy in his knowledge and happy that he knows it.

In initiating his second argument, Socrates repeats his argument that the soul is divided into three parts: reason, the spirited part, and desire. So we must remember that there exist three basic types of men: the man of reason who seeks knowledge; the "spirited" man who seeks honor and success; and the man of desire who seeks gain (wealth) and satisfaction. Remember that the man of reason possesses knowledge of the Forms, hence, Justice. Thus it is that the first man is the just man; the second, the timocratic man; and the third is a sort of mixture of the oligarchic, democratic, and tyrannical man. If we were to ask each of these men if he thought himself to be the happiest of the three, each would probably answer yes. It *is* entirely possible that each man may have experienced happiness, but only the man of reason could have experienced the happiness of knowledge because he *alone* of the three *possesses it*, besides possessing the happiness of the other two men. Thus it is that the man of justice is correct in his judging himself to be the happiest.

And it is self-evident that the man of reason is best fitted to judge, since he alone of the three knows Justice.

Socrates' third argument proves out by his making a distinction between *pure (positive)* pleasure and *illusory* pleasure (a kind of pleasure which is reliant upon an antecedent "pain"). Such an illusory pleasure might be that of eating (because we are hungry), or drinking, or, one assumes, any sort of sensual pleasure. But *pure* pleasure, such as the study of knowledge, is reflective of the pleasures of the soul independent of the body, such as aesthetic pleasures or contemplation of the Forms. And we must remember that the illusory pleasures are merely *images*; knowledge and its study are *real*. Thus it is that the just man, secure in his knowledge, is the happiest of men.

At this point in the dialogue, Socrates summarizes his argument for the just man, and he answers the other participants in the debate who had argued that the unjust man would lead the best life so long as he could keep his reputation intact, thus fooling his fellow-citizens.

Now we may behold the unjust man, who has ruined his own life by denying his reason and feeding to surfeit his bestial appetites. Nothing can ever profit him for the evils he has visited upon himself, as well as upon others. A man must learn to govern himself through his exercise of reason, lest he live a life of misery. And if he cannot be guided by his own reason, he should, like the craftsmen in the Ideal State, learn to be guided by the intelligence and reason of others—the philosopher-rulers, who will grant him justice and provide for him a happy and fruitful existence.

Commentary

Thus we have made our way through the major argument of our dialogue. We would be wise at this point to review the entire dialogue to date, refreshing our memories of the material discussed and the major theses advanced and refutations attempted by the participants. We should also at this point review the Socratic method employed throughout the dialogue, the various rhetorical ploys the speakers employ, and the systems of logic they adopt in their quest of knowledge.

First, throughout the entire dialogue, Socrates has employed argument by *analogy*, a rhetorical device that seeks to establish *similarities* between the point of the case being argued and *like* cases (for example, the similarities between the knowledge of a common dog and a

Guardian in their shared ability to discern a friend from a potential enemy). In the summary (immediately preceding) we have demonstrated Socrates' argument from *examples* of types of unjust men. And then Socrates argues the just versus the unjust man by arguing *comparisons and contrasts*. Socrates, we remember, has initiated every major movement in his argument by arguing questions of *meaning*, in which cases he seeks *definitions*. (A *dictionary* definition, also known as a *lexical* definition, usually will not suffice in philosophical debate, which requires an *extended*, or *rhetorical*, definition.) In each case of Socrates' arguing specific examples of what may be proved out to be demonstrably true—*empirical evidence*—he is arguing questions of *fact*. In Book X of our dialogue, Socrates will argue Platonic *theory*, or *conjecture*—*questions of probability*.

We are now ready for Book X of the present dialogue, which presents Plato's view of the arts and Plato's theory of the immortality of the soul.

Glossary

foot-pad   a highwayman who traveled on foot, robbing travelers; a mugger might be the modern equivalent.

inanition   lack of strength or spirit; emptiness; weakness.

Chimera   a mythical monster, usually depicted as having a lion's head, a goat's body, and a serpent's tail.

Scylla   another monster, this one the female personification of a rock, dangerous to ships, on the Italian side of the Straits of Messina, opposite the whirlpool Charybdis (which was personified as Scylla's companion monster).

Cerberus   a mythical three-headed dog that guards the gate of Hades.

caitiff   a mean, evil, or cowardly person; a wretch.

"By the dog of Egypt"   a mild oath; the "dog of Egypt" is Anubis, an Egyptian god pictured as having the head of a dog who leads the dead to judgment. Socrates probably "swears" by this barbarian god to express emphasis without being sacrilegious, as he would be were he to invoke the name of a god of the Hellenes.

Book X
Section One

Summary

Earlier in the dialogue, Socrates suggested that certain kinds of music and poetry should not be permitted in the curriculum of study for the future rulers of the State because some art did not seem to be morally uplifting, hence perhaps bad for children. Here, Socrates considerably broadens his attack on the visual and dramatic arts.

Socrates begins by seeking an agreement on *definition*; he posits the idea that artists are said to create things; hence, it is commonly held that they are *creative artists*. Thus, Socrates argues, it follows logically that we might argue an *example* of something an artist produces; we may argue the example of, say, a bed. But when a painter paints a picture of a bed, we agree that it is not a *real* bed: The artist has probably seen a bed that some craftsman built and copied his picture of a bed. But we have all agreed that a bed upon which people repose is not even a *real* bed. The truly real bed is the Form of Bed, just as something perceived as being beautiful partakes of the Form of Beauty. Only the Forms are real; the bed is a copy of the Form of Bed and the painting is a copy of a copy, an image of an image.

What is true of painters is true also of poets and dramatists; we agree that they paint pictures in words, "creating" what we call images. So when they pretend to be authorities on morality, religion, nature and all sorts of truths, that is all, simply put, pretense.

Philosophers, we are reminded, know the Forms and Goodness *itself*. Artists do not know the Truth. Take the example of the painter and extend it: Suppose the painter wants to paint a picture of a bridle. He has to copy a bridle made by some craftsman, a bridle-maker. The bridle-maker knows more about the bridle than the painter knows. *And* the bridle-maker made the bridle for some horseman, who knows how he wants the bridle made. And the real bridle is the Form of Bridle. Ergo, the knowledge the painter possesses is thrice removed from reality.

Socrates at this point tries to establish the attractiveness of the visual and dramatic arts, for which argument he adopts a kind of critical process analysis of painting and drama. Socrates points out that we are in everyday existence surrounded by spurious information and *illusory* experience which only our exercise in *reason* can correct, and that is precisely what is wrong with the arts: They deal in things illusory, depending upon illusion to accomplish their end. Painters, for example, create the illusion of depth in their works, and they can use line and proportion in the service of the illusion they are trying to accomplish. Any illusion is spurious, contradictory to man's best virtue, reason.

Socrates says that the same fault may be discerned in poets and dramatists, in that they employ language to create unstable tragic and comic characters of men and women who seem to be driven by their emotions and desires, people who lack reason. It is true that some drama and poetry is exciting, but the excitement it provokes is irrational.

Socrates concludes that the arts have a morally corrupting impact on men in that dramatic presentations, for example, provoke us to become enraged, or to burst into tears, or to laugh uproariously; they make men act like women or buffoons. We are deluded into sympathizing with the artifice of the stage, and that is simply bad for our characters.

Socrates closes his discussion of the arts and their place in the Ideal State by saying that there is no place for them. Perhaps we may allow some hymns to the gods and some poems in praise of famous good men, but the most of poetry and drama, including Homer, must be banned from the state.

Commentary

Plato's pronouncements on the arts in Book X have engaged a spirited scholarly debate that continues to the present day. Many societies have from time to time adopted Plato's ideas in order to advocate and practice censorship of the arts on the grounds that they manifest themes that are morally corruptive, that they "send the wrong message" to citizens whose reasoning power is weak at best. A totally opposite point of view is adopted by artists, scholars, and various schools of criticism who maintain that art is apolitical and essentially amoral, and that it should not be placed under the purview of any censorship whatever.

Theme

Of course a frequent criticism of Plato's pronouncements herein is that Plato presumes to advance aesthetic criticism, that he is arguing generalities, and that Plato seems to be revealed as a curmudgeon who would prefer to strip away any form of entertainment from the state. But it should be plain to us that Plato is not advancing aesthetic judgments here; he is objecting to the claim, popular in his day and in ours, that poets are good moral teachers. Given Plato's system of thought and practically everything else he has written, we can see why he would be adamantly opposed to such a claim for the poets.

Style & Language

At the same time, we must not ignore the fact that the *Republic* and several of Plato's other dialogues are permeated with humorous and occasionally malicious references to poets, Dionysiacs, and various kinds of "stage business," as when Socrates says that Aeschylus' portrayal of Agamemnon, conqueror of Troy, is that of a general who apparently could not count his own two feet. And we cannot discount the plain fact that Socrates regards habitual theatergoers (Dionysiacs) with distrust and a certain degree of contempt.

Still, there is no doubt that Plato's fellows saw Homer and his fellow-poets as a source of moral guidance; the Greeks quoted the *Iliad* and *Odyssey* as frequently and with as much fervor as some Christians quote the Bible.

Few thinkers since Plato's day agree with his theory of the dramatic arts. Plato's own pupil, Aristotle, advanced a much more detailed analysis of poetry and drama than Plato's. But had Plato lived to read Aristotle's *Poetics*, he certainly might have disagreed with its theory on much the same bases as he approached the arts and artists he dismisses from the Ideal State.

Glossary

Lycurgus   a real or legendary Spartan lawgiver of about the ninth century B.C.

Thales   a Greek philosopher (c. 624–546 B.C.) who established the first philosophical school.

Protagoras   (481?–411? B.C.) a Greek philosopher of the fifth century B.C., the best known of the Sophists.

Prodicus   another Sophist.

Book X
Section Two

Summary

Socrates initiates the conclusion of the dialogue by announcing that the rewards of justice are granted to the just after their mortal lives are over. Glaucon is surprised that Socrates holds with the immortality of the soul, but Socrates assures him that he, too, will agree once he hears Socrates' proof. And here is Socrates' proof:

There are all sorts of illnesses that can and do attack the body and bring about its demise. Every material thing we understand falls prey to its own unique "evil": wood rots; iron falls prey to rust; the body dies of the illnesses that attack it; and so on. But what is the "evil" peculiar to the soul? Of course, as we have seen, the soul's peculiar evil is injustice. But the souls of unjust men are not destroyed by injustice, and neither are the souls of just men. If a thing can be destroyed by its own particular evil (and only that), and if the soul cannot be destroyed by its own particular evil (injustice), then the soul must be immortal.

Commentary

Literary
Device

Socrates at this point employs a series of if-then arguments (enthymemes) which he builds sequentially to argue a form of argument termed a *sorites*. But we cannot at this point logically allow his argument. He cannot demonstrate the validity of the premises he argues for wood, or iron, or the human eye, and he cannot show logically that, because the soul is not destroyed by injustice, it follows that the soul is immortal. Indeed, for all we know the soul *may* be immortal. Socrates may *believe* that the soul is immortal; so may Glaucon *believe* it. But they do not *know* it. Socrates is here arguing a question of probability whose major premise we may disallow.

In Plato's world, very few people held to the doctrine of the immortality of the soul. Some of the Pythagoreans, discussed earlier, did theorize about the soul's immortality, and Plato was familiar with their arguments. In Plato's dialogue the *Phaedo*, Socrates argues that the soul is separated from the body at death and is probably therefore immortal, but another speaker says that the soul escapes the body and dissolves like smoke (a popular belief at the time).

Glossary

ophthalmia   a severe inflammation of the eyeball.

Glaucus   a minor god of the sea, who sometimes appeared to sailors to predict disasters; Socrates is apparently speaking of a sculpted image of this god which has been damaged by the elements.

Book X
Section Three

Summary

Socrates announces now in the dialogue that he has demonstrated the superiority of the just life *as a life to be lived*, whether it include external rewards or not. But Socrates sees the universe as being essentially moral, and he argues that experience shows us that the just man will receive his just rewards; the unjust man, his just punishment. The greatest of both will be in the life after the death of the body. Socrates illustrates this situation in the Myth of Er. So we turn now to the story of Er.

Part of Er's fate is that he will tell men yet alive his story of life after death. Er is a brave soldier who dies in battle. Ten days after his death, his body is taken home and laid on the funeral pyre, but there Er comes back to life and tells the story of his adventure.

After Er's soul left his body, it traveled with other souls to a wonderful place where there are two chasms in the earth and two above them in the sky. Between the chasms and between heaven and earth sit judges who pass judgment on the souls of men who come before their court. The just souls were directed to take the right-hand chasm leading into heaven; the unjust souls were condemned to the left-hand chasm down into the earth. Er was told to sit and watch the proceedings of the court, for he was to return to life and tell living men his story. As Er watched, he saw souls coming from the exit-chasms from heaven and earth; those coming from earth were weary and careworn and stained from travel; those from heaven were clean, rested, and bright. The souls told Er their experiences: The just souls had been rewarded for their just lives during their stay in heaven; the unjust, punished in the earth, condemned to wander a thousand years below the ground. The unjust told tales of other more evil men, murderers and tyrants, who were still condemned to suffer longer beneath the earth, never to be released again.

The souls stayed with Er near the chasms for seven days, and then Er and the souls journeyed to where the Fates dwell. The Fates would give the souls new lives as mortals. Each soul was permitted to pick the sort of new life he would lead; some chose wisely while others did not. The first soul chose a new life as a tyrant, thereby condemning himself to a life of misery. Orpheus chose to be a swan; Ajax, a lion; Agamemnon, an eagle. Odysseus, who remembered his earlier sufferings pursuing a life of glory and deeds, chose to be a common citizen.

After choosing their new lives and being granted them by the Fates, the souls were made to drink from the River of Forgetfulness, so that they could remember nothing of the other world and could not tell men of it. Er was forbidden to drink; his fate was that he must remember and tell what he had seen and heard. A great earthquake occurred; the souls were taken away to be reborn to new lives. Er awoke, found himself on his funeral pyre, and told his story.

Commentary

In thus concluding his argument for the immortal justice meted out to the just and the unjust, Plato is forced to argue the authority of myth because he cannot demonstrate his argument logically; there exists no demonstrable proof. Plato's myth here embraces the doctrine of reincarnation.

Thus it is that, even after death, for Plato justice is rewarded and injustice is punished. We should note carefully that each soul is granted the life *he chooses* before he is reincarnated. Plato held quite firmly to the idea that men could choose to be evil or to be good, and he did *not* hold to any doctrine of predestination of a life lived evilly or well. A bad man *chooses* to be bad.

But how can this be, when we know that a life lived unjustly is a life of misery? Why would a man choose unhappiness? Plato's answer to that is that choices are many times made from ignorance (*amathia*). The unjust man would realize the woe he is bringing upon himself if only he would listen to his reason and try to learn something. And so we see, truly, that the unexamined life is not worth living.

Glossary

the Fates in Greek mythology, the Fates (or *Moirai*) are the daughters either of Night (in some versions) or of Zeus and Themis (in others). They are the spirits who preside over a person's birth, allotting his or her destiny; they are often personified as three women: Clotho, Lachesis, and Atropos, who spin out the thread of life, measure it, and finally cut it off.

Thamyras (or Thamyris) a mythological poet and musician.

Atalanta a mythological huntress, who (in one story) refused to marry any suitor who could not win a footrace against her.

CHARACTER ANALYSES

Socrates

Socrates, whose "role" in the dialogues is always that of the probing philosopher, clearly dominates the *Republic*; it may have been Plato's intent to portray Socrates here as what Plato saw as the *ideal* philosopher trying to think his way through to the creation of the *ideal* state. For generations of men and women who have engaged the study of philosophy, Plato and his successors have provided a shining pathway to the truth of the twentieth century's W. B. Yeats' pronouncement that "Wisdom is a butterfly / And not a gloomy bird of prey." The Socrates of the dialogues is enduringly amusing: witty, occasionally droll and puckish, sometimes caustic in his analysis of any topic attempted and its attendant arguments; Socrates causes the dialogues to flourish through the centuries. And Socratic method interests us almost as much as the man's matter; if we attend him closely, we emerge from the dialogues better thinkers ourselves from having observed a first-rate thinker thinking.

As noted at various points in the commentaries, Socrates implements the entire arsenal of Western logic and rhetoric to accomplish his end of rarifying and finally fixing the point of a given dialogue. If we may adopt the Shakespearean metaphor of art as a mirror held up to nature, it may be that, for philosophy, we see ourselves mirrored in the arguments we advance and are made intellectually and spiritually better for having reflected so much and having been so reflected.

Thrasymachus

Thrasymachus, true to his name, breaches the perimeter of the dialogue with all the abandon of some sort of comic glorious soldier (*miles gloriosus*), and Socrates gleefully skewers this rash fighter. As noted elsewhere in the commentaries, we do not (and the Greeks did not) intend to denigrate the fine art of classical rhetoric (method of persuasion in argument); rather, it is necessary that we identify and refute *specious* rhetoric. And in this dialogue, Thrasymachus plainly shows himself to be a sophist, a specious rhetorician. His is a common human malady: arrogance. Thrasymachus displays his character as a sophist in the entirety of his contribution to the debate. We have reviewed in the commentaries the specious nature of his rhetoric by noting his habit of name-calling (irrelevant to the argument), his self-contradiction (a fallacy in argument), his feigned indignation (an empty rhetorical ploy, irrelevant to the argument); indeed, we might summarize a formidable list of the fallacies in argument for which he is culpable. His argument *vis-à-vis* the question of rarifying the question of justice is, we remember, that might finally makes right, in which case, *logically*, he is confuting two things: *right* and *might*. We remember, Socrates remembers, and Thrasymachus remembers—or so he says, after Socrates has argumentatively forced him to confess his having remembered.

As a sophist, Thrasymachus seems to serve as a kind of adversarial "straw-man" to Socrates' probing philosophy, but a fair analysis *does* show him to be a typical sophist. When we analyze his argument and his general way of comporting himself in debate, we can appreciate why the ancient Greeks so disdained the sophists. Thrasymachus ends his participation in the conversation by meanly congratulating Socrates on his "victory," and advising Socrates to "feast on his triumph" as though a supposed mutual effort at defining the philosophical question of justice were some sort of gladiatorial contest.

Adeimantus

Adeimantus serves as a kind of impatient, energetic, poetic foil for Socrates in the dialogue. He is impetuous and seems to seek instant knowledge. For example, Socrates frequently asks his respondents in the debate to think about the argument seriously by encouraging them to "reflect" on the progress of the discussion. When Socrates asks Adeimantus to reflect, Adeimantus habitually replies that he has already reflected, and he says that he is "anxious" for Socrates to get on with things. As a respondent in the dialogue, Adeimantus comes close to being hyperbolic in his agreeing with Socrates' arguments; with his "very true" and "absolutely" and "very good," he seems to overstate Socrates' argument with simplistic and instantaneous concurrence.

Glaucon

Glaucon, the "owl-eyed" one, is said to be him "who can see in the gathering twilight." His naming may suggest a kind of Platonic banter, because Glaucon certainly has difficulty in perceiving parts of Socrates' argument, particularly the analogies. For example, when Socrates in Book II is trying to elucidate the character of the ideal Guardian, he says that a well-bred dog has the qualities of a philosopher, and Glaucon admits that he is confused. Then Socrates explains that a family dog and a philosopher share a common trait, and that common trait is knowledge: The dog knows an acquaintance and does not attack, but the dog does not know a stranger and attacks. Glaucon says that he has never thought about that trait in a dog, which bespeaks a curious ignorance of dogs generally and a potential danger for a budding thinker.

CRITICAL ESSAYS

Plato's Flyting

In the opening of his introduction to *The Portable Plato*, Scott Buchanan writes the following sentence:

In the year 1948 the reading of Plato's dialogues by a large number of people could make the difference between a century of folly and a century of wisdom.

I have been teaching Plato's dialogues to first-year American university students since 1960, and I have watched and listened, like Er between heaven and hell, as generations of students have read Mr. Buchanan's sentence and responded with cynical silence or rueful laughter. I have met young men and women in the text of the *Republic* and the other dialogues for 40 years, autumn and spring, year upon year upon year; it has been my experience to witness the cynical silence and riotous *amathia* of the 1960s, the rueful laughter of the whining 1990s, the what-shall-we-call-it of the new century. Like Er, I have told my tale to living men—and women. And I still have hope.

Buchanan reminds us that there is a legend that Plato was a comic poet before he met Socrates, but that the story is probably false; Buchanan maintains, however, that "Plato was certainly a comic poet in the dialogues," and that the dialogues are peopled by "characters [who] are stylized to the point of becoming . . . the stock characters of comedy." And in his discussion of the theatrical machinery of the dialogues, Buchanan provides us a *dramatis personae* for each of the dialogues he includes in his text. The upshot of Buchanan's argument seems to be that, like Socrates himself, we begin the dialogues in perplexity and end in perplexity and laughter, a comedic point of view. Perhaps this is so; perhaps this is not so. Perhaps we are to exit, like Socrates, laughing.

Buchanan argues brightly that many young readers are irritated and repelled by Socrates' conduct of the argument, and they never get over it; Buchanan then recommends a traditional system for making the dialogues accessible to "stalled beginners," but he confesses that it is a flawed system. Buchanan's spirited essay should be read entire; perhaps he is correct in concluding that there is not and can never be a "system" for reading the dialogues.

Yet, there can be no disputing the fact that the participants in the *Republic* do adopt the rhetorical ploy of *flyting* at one another (that is, they engage—in a friendly fashion—in the sort of exchange of smiling insults that often precedes physical combat), and that "seeing" and "hearing" this use of language may aid any "stalled beginner" or even a seasoned Guardian of whatever academic state.

It is a commonplace of any American street scene that a minor character, generally a toady to some other major person, will appear and make some sort of humble request, ask a fawning favor. In American street argot, the response to that sort of behavior is verbalized: "Don't be pulling on my coat." The literal act of pulling on one's coat is the first "deed" (*ergos*, action) of the *Republic*; the *logos* (what is said) will follow as the dialogue is joined. The dramatic movement of the dialogue may be said to begin in the middle of things; the occasion is that of a parade celebrating a party in honor of a fertility goddess. When Socrates, whose coat is pulled, and Glaucon are overtaken by Polemarchus and his cronies, the flyting begins. Polemarchus tells Socrates that he and Glaucon had better come to Polemarchus' house for dinner; the invitation is couched in physically threatening language: "You see how outnumbered you are." Thus the flyting which permeates the dialogue begins.

Once Cephalus perceives that Socrates intends some sort of serious philosophical inquiry, he excuses himself from the conversation, at which point Socrates says that, since Polemarchus stands to inherit Cephalus' money, it follows that Polemarchus will have to inherit the responsibility for the dialogue. Cephalus, responding to the flyting, laughingly agrees and leaves Polemarchus to his fate.

The medieval rhetoric of flyting is known as "wise-cracking" or "playing the dozens" in the United States. Socrates employs it in his allusion to Homer's praise of Autolyclus; Socrates ironically says that Polemarchus is defending justice by arguing the case of a man who "was excellent above all men in theft and perjury."

Once Thrasymachus engages the debate, Socrates flytes at him by arguing the example of Polydamus the pancratiast (Socrates again implying physical violence) in order to show the absurdity of Thrasymachus' argument, at which point Thrasymachus is so flabbergasted by the flyting that he calls Socrates "abominable." But Thrasymachus gets in his own digs at Socrates, saying that Socrates argues "like an informer" who talks out of both sides of his mouth. When Thrasymachus says that Socrates is cheating in the argument, Socrates pretends to be stupid (he "dummies up") and says that he would rather try to shave a lion than to cheat Thrasymachus out of *money*. The flyting is successful because the sophist *does* argue for money. Thrasymachus subverts the logic of the debate by calling Socrates a cheater, again; Socrates flytes ironically by calling for an end of "these civilities"—the smiling insults the two have been exchanging.

The flyting becomes more bitter as Thrasymachus senses defeat in the dialogue. He suddenly engages an *argumentum ad hominem* (personal attack):

"Tell me, Socrates, have you got a nurse?"

"Why do you ask such a question, I said, when you ought rather to be answering?"

"Because she leaves you to snivel, and never wipes your nose . . . ."

And Thrasymachus concludes by calling Socrates a fool.

Midway in his attempt to define the nature of justice, Socrates flytes at his brothers in verse:

"Sons of Ariston . . . divine offspring of an illustrious hero."

That epithet is funnily true also of Ariston's third son, the man who is writing the dialogue in hand.

In thus discussing the rhetorical ploy of flyting as adopted by the speakers in the dialogues, I am not attempting any "system" of accessing the dialogues, nor am I attempting any sort of "cataloguing" Platonisms. But if any "stalled" student of Plato is curious enough to pursue the witty habit of classical insult, at least that is a kind of curiosity, perhaps the beginnings of philosophy.

When Plato Was a Child

When Plato was a child, the war into which he had been born turned its brazen face to the insignificant little island of Melos, which had been colonized by Spartan colonists who, by definition, owed their allegiance to Sparta. These colonists, who were governed by an oligarchy, had steadfastly tried to maintain their neutrality during the struggle to the death between the two great powers of Athens and Sparta. The story of tiny Melos, related by Thucydides in his *Peloponnesian War*, may be compressed in American English into a *précis*, which is my simple intent. It is my hope that any reader might take himself or herself to Thucydides' book itself for the wisdom and pathos it exhibits. The story of Melos is a melancholy footnote in mankind's tragic history.

In 416 B.C., an Athenian fleet augmented by allies from Chios and Lesbos attacked the people on the island of Melos. The Athenians maintained that it was not their intent to ravage the island; instead they wanted to court its allegiance to their cause; hence, before the Athenians devastated the island, they talked to the Melians.

The Athenians said that they knew why the Melian leaders would not let the Athenians talk to the whole populace; it was because the people would see that they were hopelessly outnumbered, and that they had no chance. So, the Athenians said, we are not here to deliver any sort of speech. We are here to ask you people some questions to which you had better give the correct answers.

The Melians said that they understood that they had two chances: slim and none; and that the outcome of the talk would be that they were to be slaves or to be dead.

The Athenians said that the Melians would do well to worry about the present and not borrow trouble worrying about the future. The Melians responded by saying that people facing death or slavery often have dreams of salvation.

The Athenians said that they knew that the Melians were Spartans, and that it was no good pretending that the Melians had not already been involved in the war, because of the simple fact that they were Spartans. And, they said, the Melians should not expect justice, because justice existed only between equals: The truth of the world is that the strong take what they want and the weak give up what they must.

The Melians replied that the Athenians might find themselves facing the same unhappy truth; if Sparta won the war, would she not pay back Athens for what she was about to do to Melos? The Athenians replied that it was known that Sparta did not ravage states whom she conquered; besides, they said, our purpose here is to save you, not destroy you. We need your city.

The Melians said that they understood that the Athenians enjoyed mastery, but the Melians had no interest in being slaves. They enjoyed being free people. And besides, the Melians said, could they not live as neutrals in the war and be friends to both sides?

No, the Athenians replied, too many of our allies think that we are letting you live in peace because we are afraid of you, when the truth is that you are weak and we are taking over your little island, since we are already masters of the sea. So you had better surrender to our wishes or die.

The Melians said that they were not cowards and that brave men fought for freedom and hated slavery, to which the Athenians replied that it was not a case of honor but of prudence, and that the Melians had best understand that might makes right, and Athens is mighty.

The Melians then argued that the fortunes of war are sometimes governed by the gods, and that as free people who had done no wrong they were in the right and the Athenians, though mighty, were in the wrong. And perhaps the Spartans from Sparta might help them. To which the Athenians replied that the Melians might look to heaven for help or they might look to Sparta for help, but no help was coming from either place.

After some more talk to no avail, the Athenians assured the Melians that their cause was hopeless. So the Athenians left the Melians that they might decide their own fate.

The Melians met and decided and then told the Athenians that they chose to die as free men fighting for their freedom.

So the Athenians built a wall around the city of Melos, provisioned it, set up a naval blockade, and proceeded to starve the Melians into submission. The Athenian troops and the Melians fought small fights throughout that summer. In the following winter, some of the Melian citizens betrayed their little island, and the Athenians attacked in overwhelming force. The Melians surrendered; they had no choice. The Athenians killed all Melian men and boys who were old enough to fight, and they made slaves of all the women and children.

Thus was justice served.

Leonidas: Portrait of a Spartan

By the time that Plato's *Republic* was published (according to Scott Buchanan in the Introduction to *The Portable Plato*), Plato seems to have concurred with his rival, Isocrates, that the Greek city-states should formally agree (in the event of war between or among whatever states) upon certain "civilized" rules for the conduct of warfare. A prelude to the fixing of such an agreement seems to be Plato's intent in his discussion of the conduct of the Guardians (Book V) in the event of internecine discord. In the Notes to *The Republic of Plato*, Francis MacDonald Cornford notes that, although Plato "expresses no humanitarian sympathy extending beyond the borders of Hellas," Plato is one of the earliest writers to stand for a rule of international law between independent states. Plato, Isocrates, and other thinkers were fully aware of the narrow escape from subjugation the Greeks had been granted at the close of the Persian war in 479 B.C.—a war waged against Persia by an alliance of Hellenic city-states including Athens and Sparta, who not many years later would be at war against each other. These thinkers had been nurtured on stories of the Persians' barbarity during the conduct of that war, barbarity practiced upon heroic Greek warriors such as the Spartan Leonidas.

According to the ancient Greek historian Herodotus in *The History of Herodotus*, Leonidas was in command of the now famous 300 Spartans who were sent, in advance of the main Spartan body of troops, to engage the Persian horde in order to arrest and defeat its intended invasion of Greece. The Spartan troops of only 300 men at arms were augmented by troops sent by several other city-states who seemed determined to engage the Persian forces, but Leonidas had picked up and accompanied the delegation of troops from Thebes, because the Thebans had already hinted that they might desert the Greek alliance and unite themselves with the Persians. In order to shore up the flagging hopes of their allies, therefore, the Spartan advance guard made camp in a narrow mountain pass at a place now made famous by the battle fought there—Thermopylae (the Hot Gates).

The reason why Leonidas appeared with only a token force was that Sparta was at that time celebrating a religious festival; the reason why the other Greek forces were so scanty was that their cities were celebrating their Olympic games. Neither Sparta, famous for the quality of her fighting men, nor her allies thought that the battle of Thermopylae would be engaged as soon as it was, so the matter stood and there was nothing to be done about it: The Greek forces were hopelessly outnumbered, the Persian forces were upon them and in command of the pass through which they were penetrating the country, and there was Leonidas with his 300 Spartans camped in front of the enemy's first wave.

Xerxes, the tyrannical ruler of the Persians and their huge conglomerate of allies, was—like many tyrants of his time and later—an unstable and arrogant person. Earlier in the war, having enthroned himself upon a vantage point overlooking his entire war host, he had alternately laughed at the earthly military might he saw displayed before him and then wept at their mortal mutability and evanescence. At any rate, Xerxes the tyrant was resolved to tolerate no insolence from the effete and intellectual Greeks who called him a barbarian, and the appearance of a mere 300 Spartans to engage his host in hand-to-hand combat must have seemed insolent in the extreme.

Xerxes was at the same time angered and intrigued by these men called Spartans, so he had the Greek ramparts scouted out. On the day that Xerxes sent his scout to reconnoiter the Greek camp, the Spartans had been assigned as perimeter guards outside the camp's ramparts. There, Xerxes' scout saw them, counted them, and then returned to report to his master what he had seen.

And this is what the Persian scout saw at the place of the Hot Gates so long ago: He saw the Spartan warriors engaged in oiling their bodies and dressing their long hair outside the ramparts of Thermopylae. He saw others of the Spartans exercising at gymnastics and swordplay and general forms of leisure activity. He saw the Spartan warriors sunning themselves. And he saw that the Spartans did not seem to consider his presence worthy of much notice.

When Xerxes heard his scout's report, so says Herodotus, the king found it laughable that the Spartans were engaging in such antics when they were, under his sway, in doubt of present peril. The Spartans were after all in a fix, and it was a fix of Xerxes' making. But then Xerxes called in a man named Demaratus who, having been deposed from a joint-kingship of Sparta, had become a turncoat and allied himself personally to Persia; hence, to Xerxes. And after the king recounted his scout's report on the activity of the Spartans, Demaratus explained to Xerxes: This is the way Spartans prepare to go into battle and almost certain death. They exercise, oil their bodies, and dress their hair. They go into battle shining.

Demaratus then warned Xerxes that the contingent of Spartans sent out to engage his vast armies was but a sample of Sparta's military enterprise, and he advised the king to attack and conquer Sparta herself, since Sparta was herself so arrogant and timocratic that no other nation would care to aid her. But Xerxes, being ignorant, ignored Demaratus' advice.

Xerxes, for whatever reason, permitted the Spartans and their allies a four-day recess from the rigors of battle, but on the fifth day he attacked, ordering his Medes and Cissians to capture the Spartans and bring them as captives to his camp. The Persians suffered horrendous losses in their offensive because the Greek allies fought so courageously in the narrow defile, employing their long battle lances to great effect. Xerxes then sent in his crack troops (his "Immortals") against the

Greeks, who proved the "Immortals" to be inaptly named by killing so many of them. Thus the Persians and the Greeks fought for three days in the Hot Gates, and the Greeks grimly refused to concede defeat. But the next day a traitor to the Greeks, a person named Ephialtes, came and whispered in the king's ear. And again Xerxes laughed.

Xerxes laughed because Ephialtes told him of a secret passage through the mountain, which would bring the Persian troops down behind the Spartan ramparts. So that night Xerxes sent his "Immortals" on their way to attack the Greeks from the rear while another wave of his troops would accost them from the front. As the "Immortals" ascended the mountain, they encountered a contingent of Greeks (Phocians) who were stationed in the Persian line of march. The Phocians fled up the mountain; the Persians advanced down the mountain to fall upon Leonidas and his Spartans as the new day dawned.

So as false dawn appeared, the Greeks at Thermopylae held a war council, where some of the allies voted to stay and fight and some voted to flee. It is said that Leonidas himself ordered the allies to vacate the Spartan ranks, but that the Spartans themselves had no intention of ducking an opportunity to fight. But Leonidas did permit the Thespians to stay and fight alongside him because they wanted to, and he made the Thebans stay and fight because they certainly did not want to. And so most of the allies left; the Spartans remained; and the day came on.

The beleaguered Greek force of Spartans, Thespians, and their hostage Thebans were now of course aware that the Persians had them bottled up in the place of the Hot Gates, and the Greek scouts coming in from the heights confirmed the case. Thus it was that, once the troops engaged on this fatal day, the Spartans sallied forth from their ramparts and flew in the face of the Persian forces ascending in the narrow pathway. By this time, the Greeks had shivered their battle lances and were fighting with swords, battle-axes, daggers, bare hands, and teeth. Theirs was the heroism and desperation of doomed men as they gathered back to back on a hillock in the pass where the Persian bowmen inundated them with flight upon flight of heavy war arrows. Immediately prior to the day's engagement, a Trachinian scout had told Dieneces, a Spartan swordsman, that the barbarians were so many that their arrow-flights would darken the sun. Dieneces replied: "These are excellent tidings. If the Medes darken the sun, we shall have our fight in the shade."

By the time the last of the Spartans had retreated to the hillock, Leonidas had been killed in action, and so had Xerxes' two brothers.

Apparently the Spartans carried Leonidas' body with them to the hill, where they all went down in a shambles together. Thus the three hundred Spartans perished at Thermopylae, and with them fell their faithful Thespians.

Shortly before the last of the fighting Greeks fell, the Thebans had tried to surrender to the frustrated and enraged Persian front line, who executed the Thebans as they tried to give themselves up. Xerxes did permit most of the remaining Thebans to surrender to his tender mercies, whereupon he branded their bodies with the royal mark, thereby granting them perpetual infamy.

As for Xerxes' capacity for tolerance and the Platonic concept of international law, it seems to have been null and void. The tyrant was so confounded by the manly conduct of Leonidas that Xerxes searched out his body from the piled dead, severed the head from the lifeless corpse, and caused the trunk to be nailed to a wooden cross.

And the rest, as we say, is history. There are many stories of men who for one reason or another survived the Battle of Thermopylae; their lives and the manner of their deaths await the curious reader.

In time Leonidas' countrymen would erect a stone lion to his memory at the place of the Hot Gates, and there too the Greeks placed a votive stone which reads:

> Go, stranger, to Lacedaemon and tell
>
> That here, obeying her behest, we fell.

CliffsNotes Review

Use this CliffsNotes Review to test your understanding of the original text and reinforce what you've learned in this book. After you work through the review and essay questions, and the fun and useful practice projects, you're well on your way to understanding a comprehensive and meaningful interpretation of the *Republic*.

Q&A

1. The main focus of argument in the *Republic* seeks to determine

   a. who started the Peloponnesian War
   b. the nature of the just life ✓
   c. who should be king of Athens

2. One of the following is *not* a cardinal virtue:

   a. musical ability ✓
   b. temperance
   c. wisdom

3. The Greek word *hubris* means:

   a. arrogance ✓
   b. greed
   c. love

4. A three-part deductive argument is termed:

   a. an analogy
   b. a syllogism ✓
   c. a triad

5. Polytheism may be defined as:

   a. a leg disease
   b. a clothing fabric
   c. the belief in many gods ✓

6. The Analogy of the Divided Line demonstrates:

    a. the dimensions of the equator

    b. levels of intellect ✓

    c. levels of social class

7. The Allegory of the Cave demonstrates:

    a. how to make a prison work

    b. how to house the homeless

    c. how ignorance may be brought to knowledge ✓

8. The best ruler of a state would be

    a. an autocrat

    b. a tyrant

    c. a philosopher ✓

9. Plato says that he loved this poet best:

    a. Pindar

    b. Aeschylus

    c. Homer ✓

10. The myth of Er tells:

    a. the story of Helen

    b. the story of Perseus

    c. the story of death and reincarnation ✓

Answers: (1) b. (2) a. (3) a. (4) b. (5) c. (6) b. (7) c. (8) c. (9) c. (10) c.

Essay Questions

1. Suppose someone had done you a wrong and you decided to get even by damaging his or her automobile. What would be Socrates' response to this situation in terms of justice and injustice? Discuss this in a graceful and intelligent essay.

2. Suppose that some members of your community objected to a book being taught in the local high school because some of the characters in the book use profane and lewd language, and the book portrayed violence. At the same time, there is evidence that some people in society do and say the types of things done and said by characters in the book. Should the book be taught? Discuss this in a graceful and intelligent essay, which reflects your reading of the *Republic*.

3. Suppose that someone in your school is teaching Karl Marx's *The Communist Manifesto*, and some of the patrons of your school say they want that faculty member dismissed because she must be a communist. Write a graceful and intelligent essay showing what is right or wrong with the argument outlined here.

4. Suppose that someone objects to a current type of music preferred by citizens your age, and suppose the objector argued that the music should be banned from society because of the harm it might do to your moral convictions. Support *or* refute the objector's argument in a graceful and intelligent essay. Your essay should reflect your reading of Plato's ideas as expressed in the *Republic*.

5. Suppose that someone murders a member of your family with some sort of a sharp-edged weapon; suppose that there are no witnesses to the crime. What sort of evidence might your community adduce to bring the unknown perpetrator to justice? What might that justice entail? Discuss in a graceful and intelligent essay that may reflect some of the ideas presented in the *Republic*.

Practice Projects

1. Choose from among your classmates students who are willing to assume the roles of participants in a dialogue like the dialogue pursued in the *Republic*. You and your fellows may choose to role-play in a variety of roles. You have already encountered sophists, logicians, ignorant and stupid people on your own campus. Prepare carefully and engage a Socratic dialogue for your class.

2. Engage in a Socratic dialogue about some absurd activity that is taking place on your campus or in your community. Invite some fellow students to adopt the roles of a timocratic, or democratic, or sophistic, or despotic, etc., person to engage the absurd topic. Or choose a serious topic and engage it.

CliffsNotes Resource Center

The learning doesn't need to stop here. CliffsNotes Resource Center shows you the best of the best—links to the best information in print and online about the author and/or related works. And don't think that this is all we've prepared for you; we've put all kinds of pertinent information at www.cliffsnotes.com. Look for all the terrific resources at your favorite bookstore or local library and on the Internet. When you're online, make your first stop www.cliffsnotes.com where you'll find more incredibly useful information about *Republic*.

Books

This CliffsNotes book provides a meaningful interpretation of Plato's *Republic*. If you are looking for information about the author and/or related works, check out these other publications:

An Introduction to Plato's Republic, by Julia Annas. Bernard Williams calls Annas' book "the most philosophically stimulating introduction to the *Republic*." Oxford UK: Oxford University Press, 1981.

The Portable Plato, edited by Scott Buchanan. Buchanan's edition of selected works by Plato, including the *Republic* in its entirety, uses the Jowett translation but includes additional notes. The other selections are *Protagoras, The Symposium*, and *Phaedo.* Buchanan's introduction is an excellent resource for students and teachers. New York: Penguin, 1977 (1948).

The Republic of Plato, translated by Francis M. Cornford. With a useful introduction and notes, Cornford's sensitive translation presents the *Republic* in language more modern than Jowett's. New York: Oxford University Press, 1942.

Plato's Republic: A Philosophical Commentary, by R.C. Cross and A. D. Woozley. This book is a close commentary on topics from the dialogue, including the Analogy of the Line and the Allegory of the Cave. New York: St Martin's Press, 1964.

Plato's Thought, by G.M.A. Grube. A classic study of Plato, Grube's book is "the best single-volume treatment of Plato's work," according to Bernard Williams. It includes a new introduction, bibliographic essay, and bibliography by Donald J. Zeyl. Indianapolis: Hackett, 1980.

The Dialogues of Plato, translated by Benjamin Jowett. Still a standard translation of Plato's *Dialogues* into English, Jowett's monumental nineteenth-century work is the basis for many later editions. Includes an introduction to each Dialogue. Five volumes. London: Oxford University Press, 1871.

The Cambridge Companion to Plato, edited by Richard Kraut. This volume collects numerous essays by various authors on aspects of Plato's work and thought. Cambridge, UK: Cambridge University Press, 1992.

Philosopher-Kings: The Argument of Plato's Republic, by C.D.C. Reeve. Like the Cross and Woozley work listed above, Reeve's study of the *Republic* presents a close examination of Plato's argument. Princeton, NJ: Princeton University Press, 1988.

Plato: The Invention of Philosophy, by Bernard Williams. First published in the U.K. in 1997, Williams' short introduction to Plato is interesting and gracefully written. It includes notes and a bibliography. New York: Routledge, 1999.

It's easy to find books published by Wiley Publishing, Inc. You'll find them in your favorite bookstores (on the Internet and at a store near you). We also have three Web sites that you can use to read about all the books we publish:

- www.cliffsnotes.com
- www.dummies.com
- www.wiley.com

Internet

Check out these Web resources for more information about Plato and the *Republic*:

Plato and His Dialogues Home Page, http://phd.evansville.edu/plato.htm—This site contains links to a biography, a history of interpretation, as well as new hypothese, a map of the dialogues, and a map of the ancient Greek world. It also provides a search feature that lets you access information about people and places.

"Spelunking with Socrates: A Study of Socratic Pedagogy in Plato's Republic" by Victor Boutr, www.bu.edu/wcp/Papers/Anci/AnciBout.htm—The author of the article states that he presents an argument "that Plato uses the dramatic context of the *Republic* to suggest that Socrates presents the education of the guardians ironically, while reserving the allegory of the cave for a glimpse of Socrates' genuine pedagogy." A quirky but interesting argument.

Plato for the Young Inquirer, www.greekciv.pdx.edu/philosophy/
plato/candace.htm—This site is geared toward the younger student and
includes links to topics like "What things were like in Plato's family and community in 428 B.C," "Plato's ideas and conclusions," and "How he impacts us
today." The page also includes links to other Plato sites that more advanced
students may find helpful.

Plato Campfire, http://killdevilhill.com/platochat/shakespeare1.
html—This site lets share your thoughts on Plato's work. The page also has a
link to a the Plato Live Chat, where you can "talk" with other Plato students
and enthusiasts.

Next time you're on the Internet, don't forget to drop by www.
cliffsnotes.com. We created an online Resource Center that you can
use today, tomorrow, and beyond.

Sound Recording

For a material regarding several philosophers, including Plato, check out
the following:

The Giants of Philosophy, **The World of Philosophy**. Narrated by Lynn Red-
grave and Charlton Heston. Nashville, TN: Knowledge Products, 1991. This
collection of 12 cassette tapes features two well-known actors reading material
on "the concerns, questions, interests, and overall world view of history's greatest philosophers." The material on Plato is very condensed and simplified, but
well written and well read, and it might be of value to students who are lacking in background; provides material on the relationship of Platonic thought
to the thought of later philosophers, including Aristotle and the stoics and
epicureans.

Send Us Your Favorite Tips

In your quest for knowledge, have you ever experienced that sublime
moment when you figure out a trick that saves time or trouble? Perhaps
you realized you were taking ten steps to accomplish something that could
have taken two. Or you found a little-known workaround that achieved great
results. If you've discovered a useful resource that gave you insight into or
helped you understand the *Republic* and you'd like to share it, the CliffsNotes
staff would love to hear from you. Go to our Web site at www.
cliffsnotes.com and click the Talk to Us button. If we select your tip,
we may publish it as part of CliffsNotes Daily, our exciting, free e-mail
newsletter. To find out more or to subscribe to a newsletter, go to
www.cliffsnotes.com on the Web.

Index

A

a posteriori arguments, 53
a priori arguments, 53
absolutes, 62
Academy, 5
Adeimantus, 24–26
    character analysis, 98
    objections to Socratic method, 65
    thoughts on Guardians, 46
age, experience of, 13
Alcibiades, 67
Allegory of the Cave, 73, 75
    versus Divided Line, 74
    hypothesis on use, 115
    prisoner, 72–73
    unreleased people, 71
ambiguity, 52
ambivalence, 52
An Introduction to Plato's Republic (Annas), 114
analogies, 86
    arguing, 16
    comparison of sight and knowledge, 69
    of lover, 61
    merceneraies analogy, 47
    permission in argument, 16
    as rebuttal to Thrasymachus'
        arguments, 21–22
    Socrates' use of, 30, 54
    validity of, 16
analogues, 8
Analogy of the Divided Line, 71
Analogy of the Sun, 70
Annas, Julia, 114
Apollo, god of reason, 54
Apology (Plato), 4
appearances, belief in, 61–62
arguments
    a posteriori, 53
    a priori, 53
Aristotle, 5–6, 90
artists, pretense of, 88
arts
    censorship of, 34
    morality of, 33–34, 38
    Socrates' attack on, 88–90
    training in, 78

astronomy, 76
Athens, 2
    political corruption of, 3
    revolutions in, 3
    war with Sparta, 2
authority, questioning of, 4
auxiliaries, 78
    courage of, 49
    role of, 47

B

balance of trade, 29–30
Battle of Thermopylae, 106–109
belief, 71
    degrees of, 71
    versus knowledge, 71
    levels of, 73
Boutr, Victor, 115
Buchanan, Scott, 9, 101, 105, 114

C

Callicles, 75
Cambridge Companion to Plato, The
    (Kraut), 115
categorical assertions, establishment of, 17
Cave, 73. *See also* Allegory of the Cave
censorship, 34, 37, 89
Cephalus, 9, 10, 75
    early remarks on wealth and justice, 13
    good life of, 13
    withdrawal from conversation, 13–14
Charmides, 3
children. *See also* Guardians
    communal rearing of, 57
    education of, 32–33
    moral education of, 37
citizens
    duties of, 46, 50
    education of, 10
    rights of, 50
    well-being of and good life for, 10
city-states, 2
    destruction of, 2
civilization, enlightened, 2
civilized state, refinements required by, 29
classes
    correspondence to human mind, 53
    harmony among, 49
Clouds, The (Aristophanes), 66
communal strength, 22
comparisons and contrasts, 87
conjecture, 87